To Stephanie
With fondest wishes
and love,

 & John

Christmas 1995

The Descent of the Child

THE DESCENT OF THE CHILD

Human Evolution from a New Perspective

Elaine Morgan

New York Oxford
OXFORD UNIVERSITY PRESS
1995

Oxford University Press

Oxford   New York
Athens   Auckland   Bangkok   Bombay
Calcutta   Cape Town   Dar es Salaam   Delhi
Florence   Hong Kong   Istanbul   Karachi
Kuala Lumpur   Madras   Madrid   Melbourne
Mexico City   Nairobi   Paris   Singapore
Taipei   Tokyo   Toronto

and associated companies in
Berlin   Ibadan

Copyright © 1995 by Elaine Morgan

Published by Oxford University Press, Inc.,
200 Madison Avenue, New York, New York 10016

First published in England by Souvenir Press, Ltd., 1994

Oxford is a registered trademark of Oxford University Press

Library of Congress Cataloging-in-Publication Data
Morgan, Elaine.
The descent of the child :
human evolution from a new perspective /
Elaine Morgan.
p. cm.   Includes bibliographical references and index.
ISBN 0-19-509895-1
1. Human evolution.   2. Children—Evolution.   I. Title.
GN281.4.M674   1995
573.2—dc20   94-49137

1 3 5 7 9 8 6 4 2

Printed in the United States of America
on acid-free paper

Contents

Introduction

A generation ago it was still common for books about the evolution of our species to be based on the tacit assumption that the archetypal human being was a male.

To a large extent that has been corrected. Academics writing about an imagined human ancestor nowadays read carefully through their papers before submission, to make sure they have not fallen into the trap of describing the creature as 'he'. That is not a mere concession to political correctness. It is a salutary exercise, reminding them that at every stage of the journey from ape to human there were two sexes, and natural selection would never favour one sex at too great a cost to the other.

However, one form of unconscious bias is still operative. If we are asked to envisage an archetypal human being, the picture that comes into our minds may be male or female. It may be black, white or yellow, but it will almost certainly be an adult. We take it for granted that adulthood is the meaningful part of our existence, and everything prior to it is merely preparation. We speak of 'life cycles' in other connections, but we do not think cyclically about human life. We think of it linearly and hierarchically. The old adage quoted by Samuel Butler is often cited but has not yet been fully assimilated: 'A hen is an egg's way of making another egg.' It is very difficult for any of us to think of ourselves as a baby's way of making another baby.

So there is a tendency in discussions about human evolution to overlook the fact that at every step of the journey there were not only males and females, but also babies, infants and children, and natural selection would never have favoured one age group at too great a cost to any of the others.

Regarding children as smaller, imperfect copies of ourselves, we explain much of their behaviour in the way we explain the rough-and-tumble play of cubs and kittens, calling it 'preparation for adult life' or 'developing the skills that they will later need'. That is strange, because it is one of the inviolable tenets of evolutionary theory that what an animal is or does is governed by events that have happened, not events that are going to happen. Only in describing the young is it acceptable to believe that a mammal's behaviour is governed by the future that awaits it, rather than the history that lies behind it.

From time to time there have been scientists who have tried to view the matter from a different perspective.

As early as 1914 P.E. Davidson was speculating: 'Infancy probably has had its own evolution.' Seventy years later, P.C. Lee and P. Bateman were deploring the fact that 'young animals have commonly been viewed as imperfect adults with an incomplete behavioural repertoire, rather than individuals behaving in ways relevant to their immediate competence and survival.'

Jean Piaget, relating his training in palaeontology to his brilliant analyses of children's development, had no doubt that 'the child explains the adult, more than the reverse.' And more recently there have been researches into maternal/infant conflict. These make it plain that an embryo or an infant has not evolved to subserve its parents' interests. In evolutionary terms it fights its own corner, and its influence on the way we have evolved has been at least as great as that of Man the Hunter or Woman the Gatherer.

The historic controversy which best highlighted the difference between child-centred and adult-centred thinking was the great debate on recapitulation. Ernst Haeckel in the 1880s advanced the theory that evolution occurs only when new characteristics are added on to the end—the adult stage—of the life history of an existing species. He argued that features of an ancestral species were then telescoped and pushed backwards, to be recapitulated in the prenatal development of ensuing generations.

Opponents of Haeckel, like K.E. von Baer, argued that characteristics may be added at any stage of the life cycle, not merely at the end. When immature creatures encounter changes in their environment, they adapt to cope with them, regardless of whether the adults of their species need to change. A caterpillar may evolve new protective camouflage—in extreme circumstances it may even change its life style and become carnivorous—while the form and behaviour of the butterfly which shares its DNA remains essentially unaltered.

Von Baer went farther, claiming that while new features could be added at any stage of life from egg to adult, the adult characteristics were never incorporated into the embryonic stage. Professor Walter Garstang of Leeds agreed, insisting with great vigour that 'Ontogeny is not a lengthening trail of dwarfed and outworn gerontic stages. Youth is perennially youth, and not precocious age.'

It is now generally accepted that the fetus only recapitulates the features of its *juvenile* ancestors. That is important. Anything that throws light on our juvenile ancestors is valuable, because we know so little about them. To quote S.J. Gould, 'Phylogenies of the fossil record are largely sequences of adults'. And trying to conceive of the history of any species in terms of adults only can, as R. Glenn Northcutt pointed out, 'lead to scenarios that are either improbable or impossible'.

This book, then, is an attempt to speculate about why our children evolved in the way they did. It set out to be no more than that. But somewhere along the way it began to burst its banks and spill over occasionally into the areas of history and economics and such related topics as feminism and abortion and the nuclear family.

I am told that librarians do not like this kind of book because they don't know which shelf to put it on. The solution is to buy two copies, and catalogue one under Evolution and the other under Sociology.

Elaine Morgan,
April 1994.

1

Is Sex Really Necessary?

Sex is not the only method of reproduction, though it has been around for several billion years. A great many living organisms—potatoes and sea anemones and tulips and marine worms and blackberries, and so on—have simpler options open to them. They can perpetuate their kind by dividing, or by budding off replicas of themselves from leaves, buds, suckers, or underground stems.

In terms of the concept of the Selfish Gene, non-sexual reproduction would seem to have a lot going for it. By that method a plant or animal can ensure that every one of its descendants possesses 100 per cent of its own genetic material instead of a mere 50 per cent. And without sex, more resources could be devoted to the growth and upkeep of the individual organism. Sex is an extremely expensive way of ensuring the continuation of a species. It has often been demonstrated with laboratory rats that the surest way of increasing the expectation of life in a male is castration. There was a long-running debate on whether or not this was true of humans. It was settled when records were discovered of a Kansas mental hospital, earlier this century, in which it was the practice to castrate patients in the hope of reducing violence. Those patients lived on average to the age of 69; the intact ones only survived on average to 56.

Nevertheless, from the time when sexual reproduction was first introduced, it became a runaway success. The reason given is that the interchange of genes between individuals results in greater variety in its offspring, so that if and when environmental circumstances change, some of them at least might turn out to be better equipped to survive in the new conditions.

However, sex is not essential to enable evolution to take place. The blue-green algae reproduce asexually, yet they have managed to diversify into 150 genera and 1,500 species. Small simple organisms like amoebas and yeast use sex in great moderation. They reproduce over and over again by splitting or budding, and only occasionally feel the need of renewing their vigour by the process of two cells coming together and fusing. Sex, say, once in every hundred generations would enable species evolution to bowl along quite nicely.

It is true that evolution in the blue-green algae has been very slow indeed. But response to evolutionary change can afford to be leisurely. The great changes in world climate happen very slowly, and rapid ecological changes such as floods and earthquakes are local in effect and seldom wipe out whole populations. Sex, as we know it, seems to be a response to a need to speed up evolution, and for a long time scientists pondered the question of why speed was so important.

A recent hypothesis is that sex in higher organisms originated as a tactical response to parasites and diseases. Given time, a plant or animal can evolve defences against most types of parasite. But a parasite is much smaller than its host, and so has a far shorter life cycle. (The life cycle of a bacterium lasts thirty minutes.) So, if a mutation arises enabling it to by-pass a host's defences, that mutation will spread like wildfire and wreak havoc among the victims. By the time the host has managed to arm itself against the new strain, its enemy may have mutated again. Sexual reproduction enables the host to accumulate, in latent form, a vast storehouse of potential responses that may not need to be activated for many generations.

For something so weird and wonderful as sex, that is not the kind of explanation that commands instant acceptance. But not long after the theory was advanced by Bill Hamilton and Marlene Zuk in 1982, it received timely support from the discovery of a New Zealand snail which has been found to reproduce asexually (the economical way) where parasites are scarce, and sexually in habitats which are heavily infested.

Once a species has wholly committed itself to sexual reproduction and evolved specialised organic structures, it is usually stuck with it.

But even that, like most biological generalisations, is not universally true. A group of plants of the family Asteraceae (which includes the common dandelion) at one time evolved the whole sexual paraphernalia, including a showy flower head to attract pollinating insects. Then, at some stage, they appear to have decided that the game was not worth the candle. They now reproduce by apomixis—that is, setting seed without fertilisation. The only reason a dandelion bothers to produce petals is that, being non-sexual, it can only produce replicas of itself; that makes it difficult to discard any features that become unnecessary.

Despite the vaunted advantages of sexual reproduction, these plants continue to thrive; when a dandelion seed found its way to North America it colonised that continent as unstoppably as the Europeans did. It seems that a living species, having spent millions of years exploiting the ability to shuffle and reshuffle its genetic materials, may arrive at a combination that is unimprovable, and give up sex for good.

Nobody claims that the human race is unimprovable, and our commitment to sexual reproduction, like that of all vertebrates, is irreversible. There are, however, several ways in which our situation has become unique.

We have become aware, as other species have not, of the causal relationship between the act of sex and the birth of offspring. Nobody knows who first advanced the theory that childbirth was the direct result of a fairly commonplace incident that took place nine months earlier, but the knowledge has been around in most human cultures for a long time.

Much more recently, we have learned how to decouple the two processes. By means of birth control we can have sex without childbirth. And now by means of artificial insemination we can have childbirth without sex.

Some of the results of these developments will be discussed later in the book, but at this point we are concerned with the normal conception and growth of an individual human child. And there is one thing about it that has not changed. One hundred per cent of the earth's human population can still be described in the old Biblical phrase: 'Man that is of woman born'.

2

Sowing the Seed

Every human female is born with around a million eggs lying dormant inside her. No more are produced after birth.

At puberty some of the eggs begin to ripen. As an egg cell ripens, it migrates first to the outer wall of the ovary, and then into one of the fallopian tubes leading to the uterus. Meanwhile, back in the ovary, secretion of the female hormone progesterone is sending a message to the uterus to prepare to receive an inmate. The uterine wall grows thicker and more receptive.

This process is called ovulation, and it takes place once a month in a human female. Occasionally, though the cycle is otherwise normal, no egg is released. Occasionally two or more are released together. The length of the cycle varies between individuals, and may be affected by the state of the woman's health, but the average is 29.5 days, the length of a lunar month.

If the released egg is not fertilised within 24 hours, it begins to degenerate. In most mammals this is a comparatively rare occurrence, because in most mammals ovulation exactly coincides with the period when the female is maximally attractive to the male and maximally receptive to him. Some species—cats, for example—can be absolutely certain that the egg will not make the journey to the fallopian tube in vain, because in their case it is copulation that triggers off its emergence from the ovary.

In human females there is no such guarantee. Ovulation does not automatically render the female either receptive or irresistible, and in human societies the act of mating is surrounded by elaborate rules and conventions concerning when and where and between whom and under what conditions it should take place. Consequently, in our species the failure of the egg to be fertilised is regarded as the norm, rather than the exception.

At this stage it is the mother's body which is totally in control of these events. Once it is alerted to the fact that the egg is degenerating, steps are taken to get rid of it. The secretion of progesterone ceases. The excess tissue built up by the uterine wall is sloughed off and flushed out together with the dead egg to the accompaniment of menstrual bleeding. The same sequence of events, including the bleeding, takes place in the great apes.

However, the present account is concerned with procreation, and therefore with an egg cell that is *not* going to degenerate. To this end we must assume that, at the appropriate stage of the cycle, a male puts in an appearance. In most adult-centred literature, as in many wildlife documentaries, a great deal of the action and the interest centres around such matters as sexual relationships and courtship rituals and how he got to be where he is. From the viewpoint of this book, all that is irrelevant. He is a means to an end, and so is his partner.

A human male is not born with all his germ cells inside him. He is born with none. His production of sperm begins at puberty, takes place in the testes, and continues for as long as he lives. Each sperm takes 90 days to become mature. It is then tadpole-shaped, with a relatively large head, a slender neck and a very long tail. When sexual intercourse takes place, seminal fluid (which may contain up to 250 million of these organisms) is discharged into the vagina.

Lashing of the tail gives the sperms mobility. As they set out on their long journey through the reproductive tract of the female, they can achieve a speed of almost five inches an hour (2 mm per minute). For much of this odyssey, since a woman is a biped, and there is no guarantee that she is going to remain supine for an hour, the journey is liable to be uphill all the way, and if the seminal fluid remained as liquid as when it was ejaculated, much of it would slide out again in response to the force of gravity. This idea is the basis for the old wives' (or, more probably, the old adolescents') tale that if it is performed standing up, the sex act will not lead to pregnancy.

There is, of course, no truth in that legend. Seminal fluid contains mucous particles analogous to those found in some species which leave a mucosal mass known as a 'plug' in the vagina prior to dismounting. In humans the particles do not form a plug, but they do cause the seminal fluid in the lower part of the vagina to coagulate within one minute after deposition, and it does not begin to liquefy again until up to fifteen minutes later. During that period, even if the woman is walking around, there is no down-current countering the efforts of the spermatozoa to swim upwards, and by the end of it they are well on their way.

This phenomenon is sometimes spoken of as if it were a human anomaly which we acquired after we learned to walk on two legs. In fact, it is not rare among the higher primates. It is found, for example, in chimpanzees. Chimpanzee females rarely walk on two legs, but they spend a lot of time sitting around with their torsos erect. In that position their vaginal canal is even more perpendicular than that of a human female.

Five inches an hour is not much of a speed, and the egg cannot afford to wait too long, so the spermatozoa may be helped on their way by the female orgasm, which is accompanied by involuntary rhythmic muscular reactions, especially in the outer third of the vagina, and in the uterus. One theory is that the vaginal contractions help to stimulate ejaculation. In boars, for example, ejaculation for the purposes of artificial insemination cannot be elicited without rhythmic pulsation being applied to the penis. Another theory is that uterine contractions may exert a propulsive influence on the sperm: 'Uterine suction', according to *Encyclopedia Britannica*, 'seems to occur when the reproductive apparatus is functioning at full efficiency.'

The spermatozoa, however, are capable of completing their journey, if necessary, without this assistance. That is just as well, because female orgasm in humans is a comparatively tardy and erratic response. It certainly does not invariably coincide with ejaculation as it was originally designed to do. Indeed, prior to the sexual revolution of the '60s and '70s it was dismissed as mythical by many of the most authoritative voices in Western medical science.

For some decades, discussion of the reasons for the undependable nature of female response generated more heat than light. Sexologists paid scant attention to the work of evolutionists, and the reverse was equally true. This mutual ignorance helped to keep alive some absurd fantasies, such as the belief that female orgasm is found only in humans, or that the organ that first evolved the capacity to trigger it off was not the vagina but the clitoris.

Since then, research has been carried out into female orgasmic response in other primates. In the chimpanzee, vaginal contractions occur in as few as five seconds after physical stimulation begins, and last for about a minute. In the chimpanzee, as in most quadrupeds, the response is normally triggered by stimulation (during rear-mounting by the male) of the ventral side of the interior of the vagina. In humans, also, that area is particularly sensitive: in 1978 it was dubbed 'the G-spot'. But since humans became bipedal the angle of the vagina has markedly shifted to facilitate ventro-ventral (face to face) copulation. At its new angle, pressure on the G-spot is much lighter and more indirect, so the stimulus has to be more prolonged to achieve the same climax.

As for the clitoris, in most quadrupedal mammals it is irrelevant. It is simply a vestigial analogue of the penis, in the same way as male nipples are analogues of female ones, and normally it serves no more useful purpose. The idea that it is indispensable to female orgasm is disproved by the experience of some of the millions of African women who were mutilated as girls by the gruesome ritual of clitoridectomy. For some of them, as a result of this operation, sex has been rendered permanently painful. But, as reported to an International Conference on Orgasm by Dr Hanny Lightfoot-Klein, others continue to find it both enjoyable and satisfying, and regularly achieve climax.

The conflicting statements made by different women about their own subjective sensations can best be accounted for by the assumption that the lessened effectiveness of the G-spot has led, as an evolutionary response, to more diffuse sensitisation of the general area, and the clitoris in particular. In the bonobo (the pygmy chimp) there has also been a similar shift in the orientation of female sex organs accompanying more frequent bipedality. It has led both to increased incidence of face-to-face copulation in the bonobo as compared to the chimpanzee, and an increased role for clitoral stimulation in the course of male/female and, occasionally female/female sex play.

With or without a boost from uterine suction, a small percentage of the sperms ultimately—after an hour or so—will arrive in the vicinity of the ovum. They are confronted with an object which is about 85,000 times greater in volume than a sperm.

They attach themselves to the gelatinous secretion which surrounds it. They secrete an enzyme which enables them to penetrate this layer. Several succeed in doing this, but there is only one winner. The first to make its way through the gelatinous zone and make contact with the actual cytoplasm of the egg, releases a substance which renders the surface impregnable to any succeeding invaders. All its competitors perish.

The victor is given a warm welcome: it is drawn inwards towards the centre. Its head swells and assumes the spherical form of a typical nucleus. The nucleus of the oocyte at the centre of the egg also converts to the form of a typical nucleus. They are now two of a kind; they meet in the centre of the cytoplasm of the egg, shed their nuclear membranes, and proceed to merge their chromosomes. The result is a joint product known as a zygote. It contains all the essential factors necessary for the development of a new individual.

3

One at a Time

'A new individual . . .' The child whose progress we are about to follow will be the product of a single birth. As in the apes and most monkeys, while it is possible for two or more eggs to ripen and be fertilised at the same time—or to divide into two before development begins—single births are the norm.

In fact, even when twins are conceived, a surprising number of these pregnancies do not end with the birth of two babies. In a study in Chicago, ultrasound scanning revealed 40 pregnancies in which twins had begun to develop. They resulted in 27 sets of twins, and in 13 cases one of them had vanished. It had long been known that, in species such as mice, embryos can be resorbed after beginning to develop. It regularly happens if the male in the cage is replaced by a strange male, which is likely to kill and eat offspring that are not his own. No one knows the cause of it in humans, but it is a perfectly natural and benign phenomenon. It is possible that if one embryo is growing more strongly, or if there is a chance that the placenta is incapable of providing for two healthy babies, natural selection has provided a mechanism for eliminating one of them at an early stage.

One reason why single births are the general rule is that humans are large animals, and the size of a mammal is among the factors that determine its life strategy—that is, how it maximises its chances of leaving a large number of descendants. Generally speaking, small short-lived mammals start breeding early in life, and bear a number of offspring in each litter. Large long-lived ones begin breeding later, and produce only one offspring at a time, but invest more time, care and energy in ensuring that that one will survive.

In 1967 Robert McArthur and Edward Wilson gave names to these contrasting strategies. They called the quick breeders 'r-selected' and the slow breeders 'K-selected'. (A possible mnemonic might be that the r-selected breed rapidly and the K-selected breed Kautiously.)

Within the primate order, extremes of these two opposing strategies are found in the mouse lemur and the gorilla. The former begins breeding before it is a year old, and gives birth to two or three offspring every six months. The latter bears its first offspring at about ten years old, and thereafter every four or five years. If a mouse lemur and a gorilla were born at the same time, and all the progeny survived, the mouse lemur could leave ten million descendants before the gorilla became sexually mature.

Even so, the gorilla does not occupy the extreme end of the spectrum. That position is occupied by humans, despite the fact that we are smaller than gorillas. *Homo sapiens* is the most K-selected species on earth. A single baby gets a larger percentage of its mother's energy and resources invested in it before and after birth than any other young mammal.

Every biological signpost—such as the lateness of puberty, the overall life span and the slow growth of fetal development—indicates a species in which births would be expected to be as widely spaced out as they are in the African apes.

The fossil record tends to confirm that throughout most of prehistory the hominids (and later, the earliest humans) were quite thin on the ground. So does the demographic profile of hunting/gathering tribes. A.R. Wallace (codiscoverer with Charles Darwin of the theory of natural selection) was baffled, when he stayed with the Dyaks of Borneo, by the fact that their population remained constant. He was acutely aware that in Europe at the same date the population explosion was already under way, and the economist Malthus had predicted that the only controls on the continued expansion would be disasters— famines, plagues and wars.

Most of the factors contributing to the way our species has overrun the globe are economic and technological, such as increased food supply, medical advances reducing the death rate, and the bottle-feeding of babies. (A.S. McNeilly calculates that 'even today, nature's own contraceptive, breast feeding, still prevents more pregnancies than all the other methods combined, especially in the Third World countries'.)

However, no other ape population would have exploded at the same rate ours has, no matter how well provided with food and medical attention. A gorilla, whether in the wild or in a zoo, does not produce more than seven offspring in a lifetime. In Victorian England it was commonplace for women to give birth to twice that number or more. There may be biological factors involved connected, possibly, with the loss of oestrus which makes sex in humans—uniquely—a round the year activity. Perhaps that was the brake that failed, and the reason why we needed family planning to restore our life pattern to something nearer the norm for the order to which we belong.

4

The Revolt of the Zygote

One of the eggs has now been fertilised. Compared with the fertilised eggs of most vertebrates it finds itself in a very propitious situation.

The earliest vertebrates lived in water and had a much more hazardous system of reproducing. Sex for fish and amphibians does not require penetration—only proximity. The female sheds her eggs, the male sheds his sperm, and the eggs are fertilised in the water, where most of them provide a free meal for any passing predator. This system only worked because the eggs were produced in very large numbers. For permanently land-dwelling creatures it would not have worked at all because the egg and the sperm can only exist in a moist medium, and the same is true of the zygote created by their union.

The next step forward, employed by reptiles and birds, was to create a little wet world for their offspring to grow in, and enclose it in a waterproof shell before exposing it to the air. For many r-selected species, parental investment in the care of the young ends there. Television documentaries have often recorded the laborious trek of the female sea turtle as she hauls herself up the beach to lay her eggs, and the horrific carnage which results when the baby turtles scramble out of the sand and are swooped upon by so many voracious predators. Some reptiles extend their maternal duties a bit farther, like the crocodile which helps her hatchlings out of the sand and carries them down to the water in her mouth.

Most birds make very good parents—often building a nest for the eggs, keeping them warm until hatched, and in some species feeding the young till they are ready to survive on their own. Perhaps the most heroic example of parental devotion on earth is that of the male Emperor penguin, who goes without food for over two months while it broods its single K-selected egg through the black Antarctic winter.

Egg-laying, then, was a triumphantly successful innovation for land dwellers—for reptiles, for birds, and originally for mammals. All mammals are descended from egg-laying ancestors. A few of them—the duck-billed platypus and two species of echidnas (spiny anteaters)— have never abandoned the habit; and in some marsupial species the fetus still recapitulates the evolution of an egg tooth though it will no longer have an eggshell to break out of.

Egg-laying did have some disadvantages, more particularly for the parents. When eggs have to be brooded, at least one parent (usually, but not always, the female) has its mobility restricted. In conditions where the mother needs to forage for scarce food resources or escape predators, she might be better off if she could pick up the egg and take it with her. For that purpose she would need some kind of pocket. In the course of time she acquired one.

The echidna is believed to represent an intermediate stage between the primitive egg-laying mammals and the marsupials (pouched mammals). An echidna apparently deposits its egg—by curving its body—directly into its pouch. Around ten days later the tiny hatchling (about 15 mm long) emerges from the egg and remains in the pouch, feeding on milk exuded by its mother's primitive (teatless) mammary areas.

Pouches provided a safe, warm refuge with nourishment laid on. Once they became standard equipment, it would have been a waste of effort to continue to encase the egg in a shell, even a rubbery one like the echidna's. The young might just as well be born alive, and in modern marsupials they are.

In the kangaroo, when the egg cell has been fertilised, the zygote descends into the uterus, where it remains for some time, absorbing nutriment secreted by the uterine wall, but not becoming attached to it. After a variable period—somewhere around a month—it emerges as a small, naked pink creature like a grub with a pair of stumpy arms, and no legs. Its mother licks a path for it from the vagina to the pouch, and the new-born struggles valiantly for five minutes to wriggle its way up through the fur, enters the pouch, clamps its mouth to a teat and settles down to grow.

Live-born young proved to be another successful innovation for the mammals. The marsupials, originating somewhere on the land masses which now constitute America, spread widely over the world and diversified to fill most of the available niches. There are marsupial herbivores, carnivores and insect eaters, and one nectar eater (the honey possum). There are marsupial runners and hoppers and burrowers and gliders and tree climbers, and one web-footed swimmer (the yapok). Some of the extinct marsupials grew to the size of mastodons. In Australia, where they met with no outside competition, they continued until very recently to be the dominant form of terrestrial life.

Up to the 1960s there was an unquestioned tendency to regard parent/offspring relationships as essentially co-operative. They shared the same ultimate aim—the survival of the species—and it was well known that in the animal world the female will risk her own life in the defence of her young. Since then scientists have introduced the concept of evolutionary parent/infant conflict. S.C. Stearns wrote about 'the concept of a trade-off between reproductive effort and parental survival . . . [The] interests of parents and progeny may conflict.' R.L. Trivers concurred: 'Parent and offspring are expected to disagree over the amount of parental investment that should be given.' And David Haig of Harvard has recently shown how maternal/infant conflict at a biological level helps to explain some of the medical complications of pregnancy. But the most dramatic shift in the balance of power between parent and offspring was that which led to the end of the reign of the marsupials.

It seems likely that the transition from egg-laying to the bearing of live young evolved in the interest of greater freedom and mobility for the parent rather than in the interest of the young. An egg is an extremely safe and stable place in which to begin growing up. It is hard to see that the embryos gained much from the scrapping of the eggshell. In r-selected marsupials, the journey from vagina to pouch is an arduous marathon, in which less than half the starters reach the finishing post.

On balance, however, the development was adaptive for the species as a whole. The marsupials reigned supreme—until the embryo struck back by refusing to be evicted from the uterus in such an absurdly immature stage of development.

Somewhere in the northern hemisphere a new kind of mammal emerged. They are called the placental mammals, as opposed to the marsupials. Placental mammals—and we are, of course, included in their number—are distinguished by the way the fertilised egg behaves once it has travelled along the uterine tubes and arrives in the uterus. It is not content to hang around there simply absorbing nutrition as if it belonged to a marsupial species and waiting to be evicted a few weeks later. Instead, it begins to behave like something out of a science fiction fantasy about a parasitic alien invader.

By the sixth day after ovulation it has developed into a hollow, circular ball called a blastocyst. The blastocyst now attaches itself to whatever part of the uterine wall happens to be nearest to it. It secretes an enzyme which starts to attack the lining of that part of the uterus, destroying the surface and then the underlying tissue, eroding it until it has made a hole big enough for it to enter and bury itself.

It then begins to grow, destroying any connective tissues that stand in its way and ingesting them. It taps into capillaries and small blood vessels, and uses the blood to nourish its own growth. This process continues up to the end of the third week of development. Its activities then become less destructive and carnivorous, and begin to be directed towards establishing a *modus vivendi* between its mother and itself. It sets about constructing a buffer zone made out of its own fetal tissue.

It spreads itself out to cover all that area of the uterine wall which has been eroded; the most deeply embedded part of it develops into a plate-like structure which will constitute the placenta. Projections (villi) grow out from the surface of the plate and serve as anchors attaching it to the maternal tissue. The space between these projections is bathed in circulating maternal blood. The main function of the placenta is to provide a channel of interchange in which the contents of the maternal blood (nutrients, oxygen, some hormones and antibodies) can pass by diffusion into the separate bloodstream of the developing embryo.

Attached to the outer surface of the placenta is one end of the umbilical cord. At the other end of the umbilical cord is what will one day be a baby.

The evolution of the placental mammals was one of the major milestones in the history of life on earth. Wherever they came into competition with the marsupials they outcompeted them. Outside of Australia and Indonesia very few marsupial species still survive.

It is worthy of note that this event was not due to any features or behaviour patterns developed by adult animals in the final stages of their life history. It was due to a change in the behaviour of the organism at the earliest possible stage of its development.

If the mother and the offspring are considered as individuals, the balance of benefit in becoming placental was extremely one-sided. The placental offspring is in clover, warm and well fed in an unchanging environment—even better than an eggshell because it is expandable—being rocked by the rhythm of its mother's footsteps and lulled by the beat of her heart.

The mother is likely to be, at least, incommoded. Through the placenta and along the umbilical cord she is committed to supplying her growing tenant with a share of the nourishment she consumes and a share of the oxygen in every breath she draws, for the duration of its residence in her abdomen. If the unborn's needs are insufficiently met by the other's intake of food, they will be met at the expense of her own organs: a calcium deficiency, for example, will be made up by withdrawing calcium from her own teeth and bones. Towards the end of the pregnancy a placental animal is liable to be a little slower at escaping from predators, and a little slower at finding food, just when the demands on her metabolism are at their maximum.

It may be observed that the female's body is already equipped with a device for evicting the trespasser if she finds its presence growing burdensome. All that is necessary is to switch off the supply of progesterone which alone makes the pregnancy sustainable, and instant abortion would result. It does not happen. A metaphorical explanation might be that the female is programmed by maternal selection to love and preserve the baby. But in terms of the actual mechanics of it, the embryo very quickly arms itself against that contingency. From the age of six weeks it starts pumping out a supply of progesterone on its own account, thereby revoking her power of veto.

The advent of the placental mammal meant quite simply that the offspring was greatly benefited. The male was totally unaffected. The female paid. It seems a little unfair, but natural selection does not function to further the interests of the individual. The fitness of the species to survive gained more from the increased well-being of the offspring than it lost from any inconvenience to the females. So the placental mammals flourished and diversified and succeeded to the position as lords of the planet that had once been held by the dinosaurs.

5

The Slow Breeders

There is one aspect of the human condition which it might be more convenient to consider at this point before embarking on the biography of the unborn. It is mysterious and pervasive, it is operative throughout our lives from conception to death, its effects are manifold, and nobody understands the reason for it.

It is the fact that, compared with other mammals, we live our lives extremely slowly. In humans prenatal development takes place more slowly, there is a longer infancy, a longer juvenile phase, and a longer overall life span.

As a general rule in mammals, the speed of an animal's life processes is roughly a function of its size. Large animals live longer than small ones, they breathe more slowly, and their hearts beat more slowly. Since we are comparatively large mammals, we would be expected to live longer than rats and rabbits and cats and dogs. Other things being equal, we would not be expected to live longer than horses and bears and lions, yet we do.

Size is not the only factor which seems to bear some relation to the slowing down process; it also varies to some extent between different orders of mammals. We belong to the order of primates—apes and monkeys and lemurs—and every member of this order tends to live more slowly than animals of the same size in other orders such as rodents or grazing animals. Furthermore, within the primate order, the life-clock ticks rather more slowly in our nearest relatives the apes than it does in monkeys, and in humans it is the slowest of all. Thus it could be said to be a continuation of an existing trend, and that in itself would not be remarkable.

But what happened in our species after the split from the apes was not a continuation at the same rate of an existing trend. It was a remarkable, an almost explosive, acceleration of that trend—a kind of quantum leap taking place in an evolutionarily short time.

We could take the chimpanzee as a representative ape, and its rates of development as indicative of what they might have been in our common ancestor. On that basis we have slowed down so far that we take twenty years instead of eleven to finish growing to our full height; the age of sexual maturity in the female has doubled from six or seven years to an average of thirteen years, and our life expectancy has doubled on average from 35 years to around 70 years.

Any attempt to correlate our life expectancy with our size has to be abandoned, because it would lead to ridiculous results. We are smaller than gorillas, but we have a life expectancy that would be predicted in an animal twice the gorilla's size.

If we compare our life span, not with adult body size, but with adult *brain* size, the picture looks more reasonable, because since the ape/human split there has been an explosive increase in our brain size, as well as our life expectancy. There may or may not be a causal connection between the two. If there is, no one has yet found a sure way of distinguishing the cause from the effect, to determine whether a large brain enables us to live longer, or whether living at a slower rate allows us to grow large brains.

This slowing-down operates from the moment of conception: the baby's timing of its own life processes falls into line with its mother's. It passes the milestones of development—such as the ossification of cartilage into bone or the attainment of muscular control over limb movements—at a much more leisurely pace than the offspring of any other primate, even after allowing for size differences. It seems to proceed on the assumption that since the species it belongs to has doubled its life expectancy and decelerated the timing of all its other life stages, it must have doubled the length of gestation as well, so that the baby can rely on staying where it is for at least eighteen months. When it is unceremoniously evicted after nine months, it is only halfway through the usual primate prenatal programme. It is more inert and feeble and immature than any other K-selected new-born.

It also departs from the norm in one other way. Although it proceeds slowly in terms of maturity and development, it increases rapidly in terms of sheer size. A human baby is 70 per cent heavier than a gorilla's at birth, not just in comparison to body size, but in real terms. A gorilla's new-born weighs on average 1,920 gms, a human's 3,290 gms. It grows and grows until its mother's abdomen is as tight as a drum, whereas a gorilla's pregnancy barely becomes detectable to the naked eye. Apes, including our closest relatives, are in no danger at all of acquiring stretch-marks. The human baby appears to start growing on the assumption that its mother's size and the speed of her biological clock are in roughly the same relationship to one another as in all other mammals. Since her life processes proceed at only half the speed of a gorilla's, she must of necessity be a very large lady and will naturally expect to give birth to a very large baby.

These unusual parameters of development—the slow growth in terms of maturity, the rapid growth in terms of size—are operative from the moment the fertilised egg cell begins to divide. They seem in a sense in conflict with one another; it is hard to see why either feature would have been adaptive for the species, and the combination of the two has some consequences which make life difficult for both mother and baby.

The only factor which links them is the slowing down of the tempo at which we live our lives, and the anomalous relationship between this slowing down and all other aspects of our evolutionary inheritance.

6

The Embryo

The people who studied the science of comparative embryology in the heyday of Haeckelism had often chosen that speciality because they were looking for what one of their number, Frederick Wood Jones, called 'the Hallmarks of Mankind'. They hoped their researches would tell them why, in the course of evolution, humans became different from other mammals.

But as they moved more deeply into the subject, some of them began to wonder whether that was the wrong question to ask. The fetuses of all mammals resemble one another quite closely in the earliest stages of development, so it was not hard to glean an idea of the blueprint for the archetypal undifferentiated mammal—a round head, a backbone, four limbs, five digits at the end of each limb, and so on. And it occurred to them that it was not the humans which had become different. All the others had become different, and the humans had simply stuck to the original groundplan.

The forelimb, for example, in many species has been modified into some kind of tool—the tiger's for slashing, the mole's for digging, the dolphin's for swimming, the bat's for flying, the sloth's for hooking onto a branch, the aye-aye's for extracting insects from the bark of a tree. The human hand is a tool certainly, but it has changed least of all from the broad five-fingered prototype with which the embryos of all the other species start out.

There were more surprising things. The embryologists looked at the foramen magnum, the hole in the base of the skull through which nerves and blood vessels pass from the head to the body. In man it is centrally placed, enabling him to balance his head easily on the top of his erect torso. This central position distinguishes him from most other mammals, and the most obvious explanation seems to be that human skulls in this respect became specialised for bipedality. But in the embryos of all the other mammals the foramen is already central in the earliest stages of their development, and moves backwards in the course of gestation. So it might be more strictly accurate to say that the embryos of the quadrupeds as they developed became specialised for walking on four legs, while the human embryos refused—or did not need—to specialise.

Thus, by the time we have explained away the special attributes of the tiger, mole, dolphin, sloth, bat, aye-aye and all the others, we are left with the human infant, evolution's supreme non-specialist among the mammals.

However, as in the case of Sherlock Holmes's dog that did not bark in the night, things that fail to happen can be just as mysterious as things that do. There would have to be some reason why a refusal to differentiate should take root only in our branch of the African ape family and not also affect our closest cousins the gorilla and the chimpanzee.

Most descriptions of an embryo are deeply influenced by hindsight. When two little knobs appear on a human embryo we know exactly what they are going to turn into, so when we have to find a name for them we call them 'arm buds'. That kind of terminology is almost unavoidable—but sometimes our hindsight saturates our thinking more deeply than we realise; we tend to try to explain everything about an embryo in terms of what it is going to become. Some of its features have nothing at all to do with what it is going to become; they are dictated by what it has been and what it is.

It begins as a ball of living cells. The spherical shape clearly has nothing to do with its destiny. There are certain morphological restraints on building with living tissues just as there are with using bricks and mortar. Cells which are dividing inside an enclosing membrane form into a ball for the same physical reason as water molecules inside a drop of water form into a sphere. Some patterns are repeated over and over again, in living and non-living things—the radial symmetry of a snowflake or a starfish or the petals of a daisy, and the bilateral symmetry of a geological fold or a leaf or an earwig or a stoat.

By the third week the ball of living cells has opted for bilateral symmetry by flattening into a disc with a streak down the middle of it. Next, the two outer sides of this sheet of cells come together to form another of the commonest shapes in nature—a cylinder.

By the beginning of the fourth week the cylindrical shape and the central streak (the notocord that foreshadows the spinal column) make it clear that it is the embryo of a vertebrate.

Vertebrates are animals with backbones, and many scientists believe they all ultimately owe their existence to a juvenile ancestor which refused to grow up. It was the free-swimming larva of primitive immobile sea-dwellers that needed to evolve directional mobility and acquired the characteristic symmetry, with internal skeleton, later inherited by all backboned fish.

By five-and-a-half weeks, tightly curled up into a C-shape with the top of its head almost touching its tail, the human embryo is recognisable as a mammal.

There are still constraints on its morphology (shape) that have little to do with what it is going to become, but by now they are biological laws instead of physical ones. For example, development begins at the front end and progresses to the back end, possibly because the instructions for initiating further stages of development are relayed by the brain. For whatever reason, the growth of the front end is always well in advance of the growth of the back end.

The fact that the human six-week embryo has a disproportionately large head is not attributable to the fact that it has intelligent parents: puppies and kittens and chicks also have disproportionately large heads when compared with their parents. The same rule applies to limb growth. The embryos of orang-utans have arms that are longer than their legs, and the 'obvious' explanation—that adult orang-utans are going to need longer arms—is oversimplified. Human embryos, too (and even human babies), have arms longer than their legs, despite the fact that by the time they have grown up, the reverse will be true. The front limbs grow first, because that is the way the embryo needs to go about its business.

The same consideration applies to the central position of the foramen magnum. The beginnings of the spinal cord are being laid down when the skull is still malleable and the embryonic head is at an angle which in ourselves would be acutely uncomfortable, involving our chins being jammed tight against our chests. In that position it would be impracticable for the cord to take a detour through a hole set far back in the cranium; it takes the shortest cut—out through the centre of the base of the cranium.

Later on, if the embryo is destined to be a rat or a rabbit, the hole will migrate backwards at its leisure as the fetus develops; if it is going to be a human it can stay where it is. But its early position does not relate forward to bipedalism, and it does not relate backwards to any distant hypothetical bipedal mammal ancestor. It is simply the arrangement that best suits the immediate convenience of the embryo.

It was easy for the early anatomists to be misled into attributing *all* early embryonic features to recapitulation, and imagining that they have something to tell us about our very early ancestors—either their adult or their juvenile stages. But it is inadvisable to jump to that conclusion before ruling out the possibility that they are merely temporary structures—part of the scaffolding, as it were—essential to the process of transforming a blastocyst into a baby.

A further example of this is found in the development of the hands and feet. When the fingers (and later the toes) are first distinguishable, they are not separate. It could fairly be claimed that the embryos of all mammals go through a stage of having webbed feet and webbed hands. But that does not mean that the ancestors of all mammals once used their limbs for swimming. The embryonic webbing is not recapitulation but scaffolding. The hands and feet begin as flat plates of tissue, and the separate digits begin to develop before the intervening tissue is discarded.

After the first couple of months of its existence, it is possible to recognise the human embryo as a mammal, but not to determine to which species it belongs. It is less than two inches long. It cannot see or hear. The haemoglobin in its blood is a different molecule from the haemoglobin in ours. It is human, in the sense that it carries in its DNA the potential to become a human being, just as a caterpillar carries in its DNA the potential to become a butterfly.

Scientists sometimes say, because all mammalian embryos are so alike at this stage, that the early stages of the life cycle are extraordinarily resistant to change—with the implication that all flexibility and adaptation are the exclusive property of more mature individuals.

They are no more resistant to change than we are. But they inhabit a different world, with no way of knowing that that world is the inside of another animal. Like any other form of life they are subject to natural selection, which means that when the conditions in which they live become different, they change in response to them. But the environment in which the embryos of placental mammals live has not changed for millions and millions of years. Their adaptation to that environment has attained a very high degree of efficiency, and they are conforming to one of the oldest unwritten laws of evolution: if it ain't broke, don't fix it.

7

The First Four Months

When the embryo is eight weeks old it is given a new title, and is called a fetus.

The timing of the change of name is arbitrary, since growth and change are continuous. In very general terms it might be said that the embryo spends most of its time laying down the groundwork for constructing some kind of mammal. By the time we begin to call it a fetus it has narrowed its options and begins to specialise as some kind of primate. As the weeks go by, signs begin to appear of what kind of primate it will be, and it is the nature and timing of these signs which may offer some pointers to our evolutionary history.

At eight weeks it measures less than 50 mm from crown to rump, with its legs folded up in front of it. As viewed from the front, less than half the height of the head is occupied by the face; above that is a large, round skull with a protruding forehead. The ears are flat against the head and very low down under the bulge of the skull; the eyes are large, tightly closed and very wide apart. It has a tail. The digits of the hands and feet are already separated and appear recognisably human—but the hands and feet of other primates at the same stage of development may also appear recognisably human. The bottom half of the body still appears shrunken and underdeveloped by comparison with the top half. There are no external signs to indicate whether it is male or female. An early anatomist, who had such a specimen preserved among his collection of animal fetuses, would have been very upset indeed if a careless assistant allowed the label to become washed away from the glass jar. Anything he wrote on a new label would be based on guesswork and followed by a question mark.

Its rate of growth now begins to slow down. In its eight weeks as an embryo it has increased its weight 220,000 times. In the next 32 weeks as a fetus it will increase another 2,900 times. In the twenty years after birth it will increase about twenty times.

The tail has already begun to diminish relative to overall size. At five weeks 20 per cent of the total length of the embryo consisted of its tail. As the weeks go by, the regression of the tail continues, helping to define more narrowly the range of species to which it might belong, since taillessness is one of the features distinguishing apes and humans from monkeys.

Our own tails have, in fact, regressed less than those of the apes: we retain all our lives a larger number of coccygial vertebrae (tail bones) than they do. In a human, the number varies from seven to nine in the embryo and dwindles to four or five in the adult. An orang-utan has, at most, three, and sometimes only two. The number is variable, because once any feature has become so vestigial as to have little or no influence on an animal's chances of survival, natural selection has no power to stabilise it.

Another skeletal sign of the fetus's kinship with the apes is the changing shape of its chest.

In a mammalian embryo of any species the chest is at first deep from front to back and narrow from side to side. This morphology is dictated by the needs of its own development in the early stages. The heart, together with the brain, is one of the most essential organs and the earliest to appear, and it takes up a lot of room in the developing thorax.

In many mammals the chest retains this shape throughout their lives; it is characteristic of quadrupeds. The front limbs have to be kept close to the rib cage so that their feet are directly underneath them to support their weight, and this tends to compress the chest laterally. It is most marked in fast-running species like greyhounds and cheetahs, but it is also true of terrestrial primates like the baboon.

By contrast, arboreal species which hang from their front limbs instead of walking on them, have broad, flat chests; and the thorax of a human baby becomes considerably broader and flatter in the course of prenatal growth. It has not gone quite so far in that direction as the gibbon and the orang-utan, but it has gone far enough to indicate that branch-swinging was included in the ancestral repertoire. Among modern African apes it is commoner in infants than in adults. Young gorillas indulge in such arboreal acrobatics for the fun of it—much as our own young like to climb trees—but their elders soon give up that practice. The same may have been true of the last common ancestor.

Further evidence concerning the degree of arboreality of human ancestors can be found in the changing shape of the fetal hands and feet. In all embryonic primates the five digits when they first appear are roughly similar in length and spread apart in what has been described as a 'starfish' shape. But all this changes in the course of gestation.

In the species most committed to branch holding and brachiation (swinging beneath the branches) the four fingers grow longer for grasping; while the thumb—which sometimes gets in the way—grows shorter and in some species is virtually eliminated. The spider monkey and many species of colobus monkeys end up with virtually no thumbs at all. This decrease in thumb size is less marked in the human fetus than in any other. In fact, in humans there is a slight U-turn. The relative thumb length begins to decrease, but this is then followed by slight secondary increase. The same thing is found in the baboon, and may reflect the fact that both species are descended from a once-arboreal species which ceased to live in the trees millions of years ago.

All the primates, except man, used to be described by scientists as 'quadrumana', meaning 'the four-handed ones', because in their feet as well as their hands the innermost digit becomes shorter during prenatal development, and its point of attachment moves backwards, so that in effect they have thumbs on their feet. In humans alone the big toe grows longer instead of shorter. At birth it still sticks out at an angle from the rest of the toes, but in postnatal life as the foot grows longer and narrower, the big toe is brought to lie closer to, and parallel with, the other digits, with a band of ligament helping to hold it in place.

At the beginning of the fetal stage, the eyes are still very far apart, as they are in all mammalian embryos. In many animals (as, for instance, in rabbits) they are destined to end up one on each side of the head, so that the animal can be aware of danger approaching it from almost any point of the compass. But front-facing vision is a basic characteristic shared by all primates, including the most primitive ones like the lemurs and the tarsier. For tree dwellers it is less important to be able to see in all directions at once, and more important to have focusing binocular vision helping them to judge the distances of objects immediately ahead of them. An animal about to launch itself into space needs to know accurately how far away it is from the branch it intends to land on.

So, early in fetal development—at around ten weeks—the eyes follow the primate path and begin to move closer together. This process continues after birth; the space between the eyes in the new-born is more than half the width of its face, but in adults it is only a quarter.

By the time we are grown up the relative space between our eyes is narrower than in any other ape except the orang-utan. The aesthetic preference often expressed for wide-set eyes, and the allegation that close-set eyes are a sign of bestial cunning, have no basis in biology. They arose only because our children's eyes are farther apart than our own and, rightly or wrongly, we associate childhood with the qualities of innocence and candour.

In these and other developments of the human fetus there is nothing as yet incompatible with the traditional view of our earliest ancestors as apes that came down from the trees and learned to walk on the savannah.

By the fourth month it resembles the fetus of apes in most ways, including the fact that they are covered with hair. The comparatively few differences in the skeletons correspond to different degrees of commitment to arboreal life. Some of the apes—orang-utans and gibbons—have stayed aloft permanently and become extremely specialised for life in the trees. The African apes are less committed: they are equally at home on the ground, and the gorilla spends most of its life on the forest floor.

The fetal evidence confirms the general belief that our ancestors quitted the trees earlier and more completely. But up to this point it is still only a matter of degree. The difference between apes and humans in early fetal life is in no way more striking than the difference between one ape species and another.

In the later months of pregnancy the picture becomes more surprising. The fetus is no longer engaged in constructing an unspecified primate, or an unspecified ape. It is engaged in constructing a human baby, and the way it chooses to set about that task takes a lot of explaining.

8

The Naked Ape

Apes are born with hair on their heads, faces and all over their bodies. A human new-born may have hair on its scalp but, apart from that and its eyebrows and eyelashes, it is hairless. The nakedness of the Naked Ape is the most striking difference in appearance between apes and humans. In terms of orthodox scenarios it is the most unparalleled, the least predictable, the hardest to explain and—possibly as a consequence—the least commented on in current scientific literature.

A great many r-selected mammals have young that are born hairless, like mice or rabbits; they are usually born in nests or underground. Even among the primates there are a few species like the loris which build nests in which they give birth to young with hardly any hair.

But that is quite a different phenomenon from the nakedness of human babies. The young of mice and rabbits have no hair because they have not yet started to grow any—it only begins to grow after they are born.

But the human fetus has already acquired a coat of fur and then shed it. The fine, fluffy hair that begins to grow in the third month is known as lanugo. In accordance with the general sequence of fetal development, it appears first on the upper part of the body, so that by the time it becomes visible on the legs, the hair on the arms may already be of considerable length. By the 20th week the head, face, body and limbs are completely covered with hair.

One of the early evolutionists of the nineteenth century, Louis Bolk, propounded the theory that *all* physical differences between apes and men are 'fetal conditions that have become permanent'. He cited 'reduction or lack of body hair' as a star example of this process, pointing out that the early embryos of all primates are hairless, and implying that humans have retained that condition. But if that were so, the fetus would never have grown its coat of lanugo. We have not, in fact, 'retained' the primal hairless condition—we have *regained* it.

Later, the Swiss anatomist Arnold H. Schultz, among his researches into the comparative anatomy of apes and humans, counted the number of hair follicles per square centimetre on the scalp, back and chest of humans, apes and some other primates. He announced that humans have the greatest number of hairs on their backs per square centimetre, rivalled only by the chimps. His most eminent English contemporary, Sir Frederick Wood Jones, had apparently been irked by the question of our loss of body hair. He seized on Schultz's data to proclaim that our apparent hairlessness is a kind of illusion and that, since it does not really exist, it is not incumbent on anyone to explain it. 'The assertion that we are the least hairy of all the primates is, therefore, very far from being true; and the numerous quaint theories that have been put forward to account for the imagined loss of hair are, mercifully, not needed.'

Schultz seems to have shared in the perception that the density of hair follicles was much more important than the fact that—especially in women and even more especially in babies—the actual hairs serve no useful purpose. When he wrote his definitive paper on the comparative embryology of apes and humans, he referred to the fact that the lanugo appears on the human embryo. But he neglected to mention that by week 36—in all but a tiny minority of cases—it has vanished, leaving the body of the new-born as bare as a billiard ball.

A similar omission can be found in most recent academic textbooks and popular expositions of the story of human evolution. Our hairlessness—that glaring anomaly—is touched on very lightly, usually dismissed in a sentence or two, or omitted altogether. To most students and laymen the fact itself is so familiar that it seems 'natural' and it seldom crosses their minds to ask for an explanation of it. The lack of discussion of this topic may be no more than an historical accident, for there are fashions in scientific controversies as well as in other things. New topics arise and become the focus of intellectual excitement, and perennial mysteries which have proved intractable are, by common consent, among professional academics, dropped from the immediate agenda. From time to time, though, it is as well to remember that there is no agreed answer to this question. If the silence continues too long, it gets harder to ascertain whether a problem has simply been put on the back burner or whether it has been brushed under the carpet.

Almost every human baby comes into the world smeared like a long-distance swimmer with a layer of grease. This whitish waxy substance is known to scientists as the vernix caseosa, which is Latin for 'cheesy varnish'. It is made up of sebum excreted by the sebaceous glands, mixed up with some dead skin cells which have been shed from the skin of the fetus, and it makes its first appearance at around 17–18 weeks.

There is nothing puzzling about the skin cells. Skin cells grow rapidly, and the ones on the surface die off and are replaced rapidly by new cells growing underneath them. That is a process which begins *in utero*, and continues all our lives. A human adult sloughs off about 8 gms of dead skin every day, a rich harvest which provides the bed mite with its staple diet. The unusual element in the vernix is the sebum. Humans differ from the other apes in having very large sebaceous glands covering the scalp and face and the upper part of the back which excrete the fatty substance called sebum. No scientist has been able to work out what useful purpose it serves. The glands in adults only become active at puberty, when the secretion has some initial difficulty in forcing its way to the surface. This is the cause of acne.

However, the baby's sebaceous glands are clearly active while it is still in the uterus and, moreover, it seems from the distribution of the vernix that they are active all over the body, and not only in the acne areas.

An attempt has been made to explain the phenomenon by suggesting that the oily secretion is necessary to protect the tender skin of the unborn against the amniotic fluid in which it is suspended. But if this were true, then all unborn mammals would need this protection. We would expect hairless nest-dwelling infants in particular to need it. But there is no record to suggest that new-born mice or rabbits—or, indeed, any non-human young—are born anointed in this way.

It has further been suggested that the vernix as a protective device is so important that the sole function of the first coat of hair (the lanugo) is to hold the vernix in place and ensure that it does not get washed off as the fetus moves around in the amniotic fluid. This, too, is improbable. The lanugo appears first, before there is any vernix to protect.

It seems likelier that the vernix evolved to protect the lanugo. In babies which are born late ('overdue') not only has the lanugo disappeared, but the vernix, too, may have vanished. Presumably there is no further need of it, and it has dispersed into the amniotic fluid, and been channelled like any other discarded fetal matter via the placenta into the mother's bloodstream, and been excreted together with the waste materials of her own metabolism.

At five months a human fetus, like any other primate, develops sweat glands (eccrine glands) on its palms and the soles of its feet. At the same time—again like any other primate—it develops apocrine glands all over its body. These originated as scent glands, and in many mammals they are used for sweat cooling.

At around seven months, when the fetus is developing from a generalised ape into a human, two strange things happen. The apocrine glands disappear permanently, from almost all over the body surface. In adults they survive only in the armpits, the pubic area, and around the nipples and the lips. The eccrine glands—until now confined to palms and soles—proliferate all over the body. In humans (and in no other primate) these are used for sweat cooling. Such phenomena, while deeply mystifying, are invisible to the naked eye and easily overlooked.

But the last distinguishing feature of the human new-born's skin is as unmistakable as its hairlessness. In around the 30th week of gestation, the fetus begins to lay down a layer of fat. From that point on the layer grows steadily thicker, and continues to grow thicker for several months after birth.

If a baby is born very prematurely, the skin may appear wrinkled and emaciated, as it often does in extreme old age when the fat layer disappears. But at full term and afterwards the human infant is sharply distinguished from other primate infants by the fact that it is fatter. As a percentage of its body weight, it has more than five times as much fat as the new-born of a typical primate such as the baboon.

The thick sheet of fat deposited between the shoulder blades makes it almost look as if it had no neck. The continuous fat layer covering its arms and hands is interrupted only by a deep crease at the wrist to allow the hand some degree of mobility. Where the cheeks of a new-born gorilla or chimpanzee are hollow, a human baby's are rounded and chubby. For other age groups 'fat' in modern societies is a disparaging word; 'chubby' is benign, because adults find these contours appealing in infants.

We are programmed to do so because they are prime distinguishing trademarks of the offspring of our unique species.

A few points need to be stressed because—as with hairlessness—the fat layer has been found difficult to explain. Hence there is a tendency to minimise its reality, so that any quaint theories put forward to account for it will mercifully not be needed.

The first point is that, unlike some human attributes, this one is not foreshadowed by an already existing tendency towards fatter babies that merely reaches its culmination in humans. In other primates the prenatal tendency to put on fat does not exist.

The second point is that the distribution, as well as the amount of fat, has changed; in humans on average 30–40 per cent of it is concentrated under the skin, rather than at internal locations.

The third point is that 'subcutaneous' does not refer only to the location of the fat, but to the fact that it is *bonded* to the skin. In other primates, deposits of fat may accumulate in subcutaneous sites, especially in torpid elderly captive species, but when it does develop it is anchored to underlying tissues (as in most mammals) and not to the skin.

The fourth point is that the human tendency to accumulate fat did not begin when people began to practise agriculture and develop a potentially more sedentary life and a potentially more calorie-rich diet. Large numbers of carvings by palaeolithic people make it abundantly clear that obesity was already a well-known established (and, quite possibly, admired) feature of humans in pre-agricultural societies.

The only conclusion to be drawn from comparisons between the later stages of ape and human prenatal development is that the human baby at some stage of its evolution became modified to fit the requirements of a totally different habitat.

9

The Sex Organs

In the human fetus the sex organs follow the same trajectory as most other features—that is, throughout most of the gestation period they follow the traditional primate pattern, but as the end of pregnancy approaches they diverge along a path of their own.

In both sexes, the organs begin to develop in the second month but, as in other primates, they pass through what is known as an 'indifferent' stage. At this period each embryo—regardless of what sex it will ultimately be—possesses two sets of gonads, complete with two separate duct systems. One set is capable of turning into female oviducts, and the other is capable of turning into a sperm duct. Until the third month the sex of the fetus is indistinguishable.

What happens next depends on the sex chromosomes. An egg cell contains a single X chromosome; a spermatozoon contains either an X or a Y. Chance alone decides which type first reaches the egg and fertilises it, producing an XX (female) or an XY (male) gamete. The birth of a male child depends on the presence, in the short arm of the Y chromosome, of a single very small gene, only 25 base parts long (some genes contain hundreds of thousands of bases). If that gene is absent in the fetus the potentially male gonads disappear and the baby will be female. If it is present, the potentially female gonads will disappear and it will be male.

Because of the 'indifferent' stage it has passed through, each sex retains, as it were, vestigial remnants of features that it might have needed to develop if the toss of the coin had gone the other way. That is why females have a clitoris (a homologue of the penis) and why males retain nipples which fulfil no useful function.

One way in which human female sex organs differ from those of the apes is a direct consequence of bipedalism. Before birth, the female is already being structurally modified to adapt it for walking efficiently on two legs a few years later. This is not because it can see into the future. But embryos possessing features which came closest to the required conformation were most likely to grow up into competent adults who would mate successfully and bequeath copies of their genes to subsequent generations.

Thus the requirements of bipedalism have, for example, influenced the shape of the pelvis: it has become more dish-shaped to enable it to support the weight of the intestines. The same factor has influenced the orientation of the vagina. In most mammals it lies in a straight horizontal line from the uterus to emerge under the tail. In bipedal humans, the restructured skeleton constrains it to make a right-angled turn and tilt towards the front side of the body.

The other striking difference between ape and human sex organs appears to have no connection with bipedality.

In all female primates at an early stage of fetal development, the sex organs are covered by two external genital folds. In non-human primates in the later stages of pregnancy, these folds undergo a process of atrophy. In all female monkeys, by the time they are born, or very shortly afterwards, the folds have disappeared entirely, leaving the clitoris exposed. In the chimpanzee they are reduced to a mere slight elevation of the skin by a thickening of the subcutaneous tissue.

In the case of the human fetus, however, the folds increase in size, giving rise to the mons veneris and to the labia, which provide concealment and protection to the genitalia.

In humans, a further distinction is added by the development of the hymen, a ring of tissue surrounding the opening of the vagina. During early childhood it moves inwards, forming a membranous fold, which may or may not be resistant enough to tear during first coitus.

The hymen is absent in all the monkeys and the apes, but it is not entirely without parallel in the primate order. It is found in the lemurs of Madagascar and a few other prosimians, so it could be classified as a revival rather than a new invention. Since the human line separated from that leading to the prosimians somewhere around 35 million years ago and the hymen has never resurfaced in any of the simians or anthropoids, this may seem an improbable interpretation. However, one advantage of sexual reproduction and the way it shuffles and reshuffles the genes is that redundant chromosomal instructions can be stored in latent form over vast stretches of time as a kind of contingency reserve, and reactivated as conditions change. Fish, for example, have had two eyes for around 400 million years, yet in some species, altering their environment by adding a touch of magnesium chloride to the water in which they are developing can result in a fish with the long-extinct ancestral attribute of a single central eye.

In human males, the sex organ shares one characteristic with an even more remote relative than the lemurs, namely the tarsier. In this case what they have in common is the absence of a feature rather than the presence of one. Apes and monkeys and lemurs all have a bone in the penis; men and tarsiers do not.

The cover-up tendency indicated by the development of the labia and the hymen in females finds a faint echo in the prenatal development of the male genitalia. When the penis first evolves it has no covering; later, as in other mammals, the foreskin (the prepuce) arises in the form of skin folds at the base, and gradually extends down the sides. There is a good deal of variety between different species in respect of how far down this covering extends. In humans, by the time the baby is born, it not only completely covers the organ but in 96 per cent of boys it is non-retractable. Normally it undergoes spontaneous separation as time goes by; by the age of three it only remains non-retractable in ten per cent of boys and by five years that is reduced to five per cent.

Human males after puberty were long considered to be top of the primate league in respect of penis length relative to body size. Occasional attempts were made to correlate this in some way with social factors such as male hierarchies or degrees of polygamy, on the assumption that the penis was an epigamic adornment designed to attract females or intimidate other males.

On the reasonable assumption that changes in the design of the genital organs co-evolved in males and females, it seems likelier that increased penis length is a response to inaccessibility of the vagina due to the labia and the change to face-to-face copulation, consequent on bipedalism. In the only primate which exceeds *Homo* in relative penis size—the bonobo—there has also been modification in the female anatomy, and face-to-face copulation is a frequent practice.

Breasts are described as 'secondary sexual characteristics'. Again there is a tendency in the case of our own species to account for the way they have evolved in terms of display, rather than in terms of their primary function of providing nourishment.

All mammals have milk glands. That is the definitive sign of which order they belong to. (*Mamma* is Latin for breast.) At an early embryonic stage milk strips develop, running down each side of the ventral surface of the body. In monotremes, like the platypus, the milk simply seeps out onto the surface of the skin, rather as sweat does, and is licked off by the young. In more advanced (eutherian) mammals it is channelled through nipples. These may be arranged in rows, in species like pigs or dogs which have large litters. In K-selected species the teats are fewer in number and concentrated either at the front or back end of the body. In the majority of terrestrial mammals they are situated, as in horses and sheep, towards the hind end of the body. It is a suitably well-protected area, not vulnerable to head-on attacks from predators or rivals, and barricaded by the spine and the hind limbs. In grazing animals it is high enough from the ground to allow a fawn or a colt to stand underneath and suckle. At least one small primitive primate, the aye-aye, has nipples in the same place.

Monkeys and apes, however, have developed paired nipples at the opposite end of the milkstrip, at chest level (pectoral). It would be difficult for an average-sized monkey to balance quadrupedally on a branch while its offspring stood underneath it and suckled, so primates tend to sit upright while suckling their young, and if the nipples were in the same place as the sheep's, the monkey's baby would have had to be held upside-down to nurse.

At an early point in the embryonic stage, the nipples of monkeys and apes and humans are all at the same level on the chest. Later, however, in all the monkeys and apes they move a little higher, nearer to shoulder level. Sometimes, as in the gelada, they also move closer together (an infant gelada can suckle from both nipples at the same time); in the New World monkeys and the orang-utan, they move farther apart and are situated near the armpits. According to primatologist J.H. Napier, this ensures that they can be reached by the young clinging to the mother's back.

But in all non-human anthropoids the nipples, whether close together or far apart, always move upwards during gestation. In humans the opposite is true. During the third, fourth and fifth fetal months the nipples move gradually downwards. This migration continues for a while after birth so that in adults the nipples are relatively lower than a new-born's.

This curious anomaly is probably due to two factors: the fact that humans lost their body hair, and the fact that their babies are born in such a helpless state. A young chimpanzee or gorilla from the time it is born can cling tightly to its mother's fur. When she puts it to the breast it can hang on there while it suckles. The human new-born has no maternal hair to cling to, and it is born in such a helpless state that it cannot even hold its head up. Consequently, the mother finds it most convenient to hold the baby cradled in her arms—as it grows heavier, in her lap—and bring the nipple down to its mouth rather than vice versa.

This process is made somewhat easier by the prenatal downward migration of the nipples, and is presumably the reason why it takes place. It is further considerably aided by the development after puberty of the human breast, which ensures that the nipple is no longer anchored tightly to the ribs, as in monkeys. The skin of the breast around the nipple becomes more loosely-fitting to make it more manoeuvrable, leaving space beneath the looser skin to be occupied by glandular tissue and fat. Adult males find the resulting species-specific contours sexually stimulating, but the instigator and first beneficiary of the change was the baby.

10

Brain Growth—the Problem

Some readers may feel that the story so far has been like a performance of *Hamlet* without the Prince of Denmark. The ultimate hallmark of humanity is often felt to be not the naked skin nor the erect stance nor the opposable thumb, but the mighty brain. And one aspect of brain growth is that it led to a sharper potential conflict between the interests of mother and baby than any event since the evolution of the placenta—a conflict only resolved by some ingenious and unprecedented compromises.

Humans are primates, and the primates—lemurs and monkeys and apes—differ from all the other orders of mammals in that a new-born primate has a larger brain in relation to body size than the new-born of other orders such as rodents or carnivores or grazing mammals.

One result of this is that some small monkeys find the process of giving birth laborious because there is such a tight fit between the mother's pelvis and her baby's skull. In many of the New World monkeys the head breadth is larger than the diameter of the pelvic inlet and if the new-born tried to enter the world head first (crown presentation—the commonest type in human childbirth) it could not successfully pass through the pelvic canal. But the dimensions from the top of the head to the jaw are smaller, and the head can be tilted backwards (dorsiflexed)—emerging face first. Also, the pelvic ring can be slightly enlarged by stretching the ligaments which normally hold the pelvic bones tightly together. Even with the aid of these manoeuvres, labour is strenuous and delivery is difficult. Still births are quite frequent. The problem is most acute in the squirrel monkey, in which the new-born has an unusually big head. Squirrel monkey mothers giving birth have been observed to grasp the infant's head, apparently in an attempt to pull it out. As soon as the infant's hands are free, it grasps the mother's fur tightly as if trying to help in extricating itself. In this species it has been calculated that—at least in zoos—only about half of the pregnancies result in a live infant.

Larger monkeys have an easier time, and the great apes have the easiest time of all. That is because, within any order of mammals, when the body size increases the brain size does not keep pace with it, but only increases 75 per cent as much as the overall size. So a monkey four times the size of a squirrel monkey has a brain only three times as big, and since this is equally true of its baby's brain at birth, birth is a much less hazardous business.

Consequently, in the great apes there is a comfortable clearance between the new-born's skull and the mother's pelvis. Childbirth in the gorilla is comparatively quick and trouble free. Sometimes the baby fails to survive, but that is not due to the hazards of being born. It happens most frequently when the females were themselves reared in captivity, and have had no opportunity of acquiring the skills of mothercraft by observing their own mothers or other older females.

Human females are roughly within the same size range as the female great apes. Gestation length (about 266 days) is the same as in the orang-utan, and not much longer than in the African species (chimpanzee about 230 days, gorilla 260 days). So it might be expected that women also would have no obstetric problems. As we know, that is not the case. In *Homo sapiens* obstetric conditions regularly arise not only hazardous to the life of the infant but—

barring surgical intervention—hazardous to the life of the mother also.

It would be natural to jump to the conclusion that that is because our babies have much bigger skulls relative to their body size than do the new-born gorillas or chimpanzees. But that is not true. The relative cranial capacity of a new-born human (9.9 per cent of its body size) is only slightly larger than that of a new-born chimpanzee (9.7 per cent). And there are a few primates (the spider monkey and a couple of species of macaques) in which the heads of new-born infants are relatively bigger than in human babies. Most of the impressive expansion in human brain size does not take place until after birth.

What a woman produces, compared with the apes, is not a similar-sized baby with an extra large head, but a baby twice as large, and she does this without appreciably lengthening the period of gestation. Compared with a chimpanzee, she spends 16.7 per cent extra time producing a baby which is 92.2 per cent larger. Somewhere along the line of evolution, human females have opted—or been compelled, or been enabled—to invest a vastly increased proportion of their physical resources in the production of each child before it is born.

Between the time of the split from the apes five million years ago and our own time, three things have happened which made us unique. One was bipedalism, one was brain growth, and the third was the slowdown in our rates of metabolism. They did not all occur at the same time or at the same rate, and one thing important to get clear is the sequence of events.

One of the earliest was the change from walking on four legs to walking on two. Proof of this was found in the skeleton of 'Lucy', the fossil hominid discovered at Hadar in 1974 by Don Johanson and Tim White. Lucy was small—only about 3 ft 5 ins high—and had a small brain, but her pelvis showed clear signs of adaptation to bipedal locomotion. And some fossil remains of Lucy's species

(*Australopithecus afarensis*) date back to almost four million years ago.

It is also possible to work out very approximately when the increase in brain size began. Earlier in this century it used to be thought that the large brain was the earliest of the distinctively human features to be acquired: that is why the Piltdown hoax fooled so many people for so many years. The discovery of the skeleton AL 288-1 (the hominid known as Lucy) came as a shock to scientists because although Lucy was already bipedal, her brain was described as being no bigger than that of a modern chimpanzee.

That comment is literally true, but misleading for two reasons. Lucy was smaller than any of the great apes, and would be expected—other things being equal—to have a *smaller* brain. Also, because of a general trend to brain expansion over time in all primates, any ape contemporary with Lucy would have had a smaller brain than a modern one. Once these scaling effects are taken into consideration, it becomes clear that Lucy's relative brain size had already begun to increase.

Robert Martin, then Professor of Anthropology at University College London, drew attention to these facts in an influential speech to the American Museum of Natural History in 1982. He calculated that between the split from the apes and the time of the australopithecines, Lucy's relative brain size may have increased by around 30 per cent. He therefore concluded that, 'Expansion of human brain size, relative to body size, probably began about five million years ago, if not earlier.' However, although the beginning of brain growth dates back a long way, it proceeded quite slowly between five million and two-and-a-half million years ago, when it entered a phase of very rapid expansion.

The third feature (the slowing down of all our life stages) probably began around two-and-a-half million years ago, at the same time as brain growth speeded up. This was calculated by Timothy Bromage and Christopher Bean, who conducted research into the rates of growth of teeth in immature fossils. From this they deduced that in the early hominids like Lucy, the rate of maturation of the young was more similar to that of the apes than of modern humans. And this was still broadly true of *Homo habilis*, the first tool-making species, over a million years later. Not until the time of *Homo erectus* were there any clear signs that the life cycle was proceeding at a slower pace.

If, then, we are looking for causal connections, it seems clear that the slowing down could not have been the cause of bipedalism or brain growth, but it could have been a result of one of these or, more probably, of the combination between the two. The increasing incompatibility between the pressures for efficient bipedalism (a narrow pelvis) and the pressures for large-brained infants (a wide pelvis) could have escalated to a critical point at which something had to give. The only large mammal in which relative brain size rivals our own is the dolphin, but the dolphin faces no obstetric constraints because it has lost its hind limbs and the pelvic bones are reduced to vestiges.

One of the unsolved questions is why the brain began to grow. This used to elicit a widely accepted, if simplistic, answer: the hominids grew bigger brains because—in order to survive on the savannah—they needed greater intelligence. This argument is based on three unjustified assumptions. Firstly, that a primate on the savannah needs more intelligence than a primate in the trees. Secondly, that greater intelligence correlates with a bigger brain. Thirdly, that any species which would benefit from a bigger brain would automatically acquire one.

There is no evidence that any of the successful species of savannah mammals have more intelligence or bigger brains than their forest-dwelling relations. The need to co-operate on the hunt was once alleged to demand a bigger brain, but the wolf's cranium is not relatively any bigger than the solitary dingo's. Tool-making and tool-using were other suggested explanations, but an ape's brain is already big enough for this purpose.

Among the most intelligent apes to be studied to date is the bonobo (pygmy chimpanzee) called Kanzi. He was not reared in a house like a human child, but brought up in semi-natural woodland. However, he had plenty of attention and stimulation from human companions, and by the time he was five years old his understanding of English sentences was extensive. He could respond to combinations of words he had never heard before. E.S. Savage Rumbaugh filmed him using a stone to crack a nut, which he had learned to do by watching a chimpanzee doing it on television. In Kanzi, this was of course merely imitation—a cultural acquirement rather than an evolutionary leap forward.

But the same thing was broadly true of early humans. The Acheulian handaxe, a hand-held cutting tool first produced by early humans in Africa, was widely imitated and the use of it spread over Africa, Europe, the Near East, and into Asia as far as Calcutta. It is true that improvement in technique occurred as time went by, but only very slowly. It took 500,000 years—during which brain expansion was proceeding at an unprecedented rate—to perfect the design.

On the second point, despite persistent attempts, no one has succeeded in establishing any correlation between brain size and intelligence. Raymond Dart, the South African anatomist who discovered an early hominid known as the Taung baby, pointed out that the skulls of normally functioning modern humans can vary in capacity from 790 cc to 2,350 cc. In no sphere of life can competence or success be related to the size of the brain. The poet Byron's brain weighed 2,380 gms and the poet Walt Whitman's only 1,282 gms. George Cuiser, the French biologist, and Johann Dollinger, the German anatomist, prospered in their respective professions though one had a brain weighing 1,830 gms and the other 1,207 gms. Women, on

average, have smaller brains than men, but the neurons
are more densely packed in the cerebral cortex than they
are in men's brains; the total average number of neurons
is not detectably different. And though *Homo sapiens* has
a brain about three-and-a-half times the size of a chimpanzee's, he has only one-and-a-quarter times as many
cortical neurons.

On the third point, it is now recognised that growing a
bigger brain was a particularly costly investment—much
more so than, for example, the evolution of longer legs.
The metabolic demands of growing and maintaining a
large brain are disproportionately great when compared
with the creation and maintenance of other tissues of the
body. In an adult human the brain represents only about
two per cent of body weight, yet it consumes some 18 per
cent of the body's energy.

Growing a larger brain, then, does not depend solely
on whether or not a bigger brain would serve some useful
purpose. The extra metabolic resources for this expensive
investment would initially have to be supplied by the
mother throughout the periods of pregnancy and lacta-
tion. In the larger primates this means over a period of
years. It is not surprising that, as pointed out by R.D.
Martin, the degree of relative brain growth within a mammalian order frequently correlates with the nutritional
value of the maternal diet: '[There is] clear evidence of a
particularly intimate connection between the gestational
processes (including the mother's metabolic capacity) and
fetal brain growth, thus singling out the brain as an organ
of special significance in the maternal/fetal relationship.'

In order to fuel the increased gap between the relative
brain size in the hominids and the apes, increased energy
resources must have become available to the hominid
mothers, presumably through a change of diet and/or
environment. The probable nature of that change will be
discussed in a later chapter.

The fetus's environment was modified in only one

respect. It was still floating safely in its confined space, insulated against any sudden changes of temperature or climate. But at some point the maternal metabolic turnover was increased; the blood flowing through the placenta of every hominid fetus contained a richer and more dependable supply of nutrients, and nothing could prevent the fetus from taking advantage of it. Other things being equal, better-fed mothers produce bigger babies, and bigger babies are more likely to survive. But if this process continues beyond a certain point, there may be a conflict of interest between the mother and the baby. If her offspring are too big, they constitute too great a drain on her resources. She will reproduce less often and leave fewer dependents.

Thus, as David Haig points out, genetic conflict can be said to exist between maternal and fetal genes. 'Fetal genes will be selected to increase the transfer of nutrients to the fetus, and maternal genes will be selected to limit transfers in excess of some maternal optimum.'

And there is another factor to be considered, a factor which has not featured prominently in this narrative since the beginning—the father. The father is on the baby's side. It is in his interest for his own offspring to be large and lusty; he is less concerned that the mother safeguard her resources to produce future children. (She knows they will be hers; he has no guarantee that they will be his.)

In mice it has been found that in the embryos, the gene for a certain growth hormone (1GF-11) is active only when it comes from the father. The copy of the gene inherited from the mother is silent. Those who inherit the active gene from their father are 30 per cent bigger.

However, there comes a point where the interests of mother and baby begin to coincide. If the increased size of the fetus—and particularly its head—continues to the point where it cannot pass through the pelvic ring, neither of them can win. It may well be that the long period of very slow growth in encephalisation (relative brain size increase) between four million and two-and-a-half million years ago meant that this sticking point was imminent and, until a solution was found, there was stalemate.

11

Brain Growth—the Solution

On the face of it the problem does not seem to have been unique. It had much in common with the situation that arises when a large male animal is mated with a small female animal of the same species. The classic illustration of this was an experiment consisting of cross-mating between a pair of large Shire horses and a pair of small Shetland ponies. It gave rise to no difficulties at all. The Shire mother gave birth to a large foal sired by the little Sheltie male; the Shetland mare produced a small foal fathered by the large Shire stallion. After birth the small foal grew more quickly, and the large one slowed down, so that after a few months both offspring were the same size, and remained so for the rest of their lives.

On this analogy it would seem that there is a perfectly good mechanism already available to enable a small mother to produce a potentially large baby which will put on a spurt after it is born. However, it seems that the tailoring of the baby to fit the space available is conditioned by the size of the mother's abdomen, not by the size of her pelvic outlet. In most quadrupeds, as with the horses, a species with a large abdomen will also have a large pelvis. It was bipedalism that threw a spanner in the works.

One method of responding to the problem is by developing pelvic dimorphism—the female pelvis becomes differently shaped from the male's. This was the solution resorted to by the New World monkeys. The ones which show the greatest degree of pelvic dimorphism are the ones with relatively bigger heads. This course was also adopted by our ancestors. Pelvic dimorphism—which is trifling in the African apes—is greater in *Homo sapiens* than in any other primate except the squirrel monkey. But there was a limit to how far it could go. The main effect was to insulate the male from the problems of the female rather than to solve these problems.

Another solution is adopted by the marmoset: it is to divide the fetal cargo into two and produce twins every time. In a species with such a tight brain/pelvis ratio, the two smaller offspring can be delivered more easily than one large one. For whatever reason the hominids did not attempt this solution, and twinning has not become the norm in our species.

Two other compromises were introduced—one by the mother, making the pelvic ring temporarily larger, and the other by the baby, making its skull temporarily smaller.

The first of these was achieved by acquiring a small degree of elasticity. At the front of pelvic ring where the pelvic bones meet, the join between them is tightly welded in almost all adult mammals, and also in male humans. But in the females of *Homo sapiens* and the squirrel monkey, it has the capacity to open slightly during childbirth, and close again after it.

The baby's counter-concession was even more ingenious. Before birth the separate bones of the skull are joined along lines known as sutures, and at points where three bones meet there are little gaps called fontanelles, which close after birth.

In humans one of these (called the anterior fontanelle) is not a little gap but quite a big one—a diamond-shaped aperture about an inch in diameter towards the front of the top of the head. When the baby is born, this aperture is covered only with skin, and the brain can be seen pulsing beneath it. When the bones of the skull are compressed too tightly during its transit through the pelvis, the fontanelle is big enough to enable them to some extent to slide over one another, and thus decrease the overall dimensions of the cranium to ease its passage. It is the only stage of our development at which we really do need a hole in the head. At about three months after birth, the bones surrounding it begin to grow inwards and meet, and in over 90 per cent of children the fontanelle is obliterated by the age of two.

However, the permanent solution to the problem was a kind of *coup d'etat* by the mothers, who took to evicting their babies prior to the stage of maturation which constitutes 'full term' in monkeys and apes. This was not at all the same device as that employed by the Shetland pony; her foal was delivered mature and perfectly formed, although miniaturised. The process in the hominids was something more like spontaneous abortion at a late stage of gestation. It must have begun by very slow and gradual stages, for normally, in the wild, infants born prematurely would not survive. Perhaps the infants were aided by their subcutaneous fat layer, which would provide some degree of insulation against friction as well as against cold.

Once this process had begun, it continued. The baby continued its drive to grow larger; the mother countered by evicting it at an earlier and earlier stage of its development without shortening the period of gestation, so that its prenatal growth was able to slow down. At each step in this process, the willingness of the mothers to care diligently for these increasingly helpless offspring would become greater, because the mothers who failed to respond in this way would leave no descendants.

There is no other way to explain the transition to the human condition from that found in all other primates. Adolf Portmann in the 1940s was the first to concentrate his attention on this anomaly; normally in the litters of rapidly breeding and r-selected mammals we find very underdeveloped, helpless, naked, blind young—scientifically described as 'altricial'. In highly evolved K-selected, slow-developing mammals the young are born in a very advanced state ('precocial'). Human babies are the glaring exception. They have relapsed into a helpless and undeveloped state; scientists describe them as 'secondarily altricial'. There is no reason to suppose that this was true of the common ancestor of apes and men: it is a condition that must have developed within the last five million years, most probably within the last three million, and it cannot have happened overnight.

Portmann's analysis was largely ignored for a few decades, but the essential truth of it is now recognised. Its recognition was aided when in 1977 Stephen Jay Gould was prepared to say, 'I suspect that Portmann is approximately right in arguing that we would spend 21 months *in utero* if our retardation in gestation matched the slowdown in our other systems.'

The consequences of this solution to the obstetric dilemma were immense and far-reaching. The brakes on relative brain growth were removed. The rapid growth of brain size—normally only found in unborn mammals—was able to continue unchecked on the safe side of the pelvic bottleneck. The slow, halting rate of increase in cranial capacity that began five million years ago gave way to the phase of very rapid expansion during which the human brain almost doubled in size between *Homo habilis*—about two-and-a-half million years ago—and modern humans. A similar burst of expansion occurs in every individual lifetime: between birth and the age of four years the human brain triples in size.

This scenario might also explain why brain growth came to a halt around 10,000 years ago. There are biological limits to most things. In humans the crisis point of birth has been pushed back a long way, to an earlier stage of physiological development than in any other K-selected species, and babies have adapted in their own way to cope with this unprecedented situation.

Perhaps about 10,000 years ago a point was reached

when to push it back any farther would have been counter-productive. Babies, collectively, have one very strong card they can play: they can die. By means of natural selection that would hand the initiative back to them and enable them to say, in respect of slow-down and brain growth simultaneously: 'Thus far, and no farther'.

12

Preparing to Come Out

In the last eight weeks of gestation the baby is beginning to prepare for life on the outside.

Its demands on its mother's resources are now at their maximum. It has access via the placenta to its mother's arterial blood, and can release hormones and other substances directly into her circulation. David Haig has suggested that this could be the explanation for some of the disorders of pregnancy. Placental hormones, acting to maintain high glucose levels in maternal blood, could in some circumstances lead to gestational diabetes; and an attempt by a poorly nourished fetus to increase its supply of nutrients by increasing maternal blood pressure could be the cause of pre-eclampsia.

By now there is no difficulty at all in recognising to which species it belongs. It is a human baby, and every day that passes increases the likelihood that, if born, it will survive. Its head, which at three weeks constituted half the length of its body, now constitutes only a quarter of it. Its eyes, once closed like a kitten's, are open. It can see and hear. It reacts to sudden loud noises, and responds to such light as reaches it—the kind of red glow you see if you put your hand over an electric torch and switch it on.

It has fingernails which its admirers will exclaim over for their miniaturised perfection. It has muscles. Compared with those of other prenatal primates they are very feeble, but it can use them to kick and move its arms about. If, in the course of these aimless movements, its thumb finds its way to its mouth, it will suck it. Since it enjoys sucking things, that originally random movement will tend to be repeated more often—which is another way of saying it can learn. Some thumb-sucking babies have become hooked on the habit before they were born.

Preparations for being born are not the same in human babies as they are in other primates. An ape or monkey at this stage is hurrying to grow a fur coat that will become longer and thicker after it is born. It is also hurrying to strengthen the muscles of its hands and arms and fingers so that it can cling to its mother's fur, and harden its bones so that they can support its weight. In a macaque, by the time it is three-quarters through gestation, the limb bones have become ossified to an extent that the human child will not match until years later.

A human child has different priorities. It is true that during the first week of life, if you put your fingers into its palms it will grasp them strongly enough to support its own weight if you lift it. Its infant ancestors were arboreal enough for that grasp-reflex to be a matter of life and death. It was so deeply implanted that five or six million years have not been sufficient time to eradicate it.

But in most respects it is under no pressure to become physically agile: there will be plenty of time for that later. As with other mammals, there is no urgency for its teeth to grow. They are already formed in the gums, and have been calcifying for the past three months, but the baby has evolved to feed on milk, so it will be adequate for its own purposes—and more comfortable for its mother—if the teeth do not break the surface until around seven months after its birth.

There are two things which it treats as urgent—one of them a human anomaly, the other common to all mammals. The anomalous one is the subcutaneous layer of fat. Building this up consumes a high proportion of the metabolic resources allotted to it in the final weeks of gestation. No other primate fetus seems to consider that a sensible way of investing its energy prior to the great challenge of emerging into the unknown. Primate babies are all quite happy to be born light and easily portable—all, that is, except *Homo sapiens*.

The other urgent matter is common to all mammals. Ever since conception the fetus has been breathing—in the sense of taking in oxygen and giving out carbon dioxide— through its navel, via the umbilical cord and the placenta. All life began in water; the human embryo in its earliest stages still has gill-slits, and for the first nine months of our existence water is still our environment. For the first animals to emerge onto dry land it took millions of years to evolve an efficient mechanism for extracting oxygen from air instead of from water.

The fetus has inherited this mechanism—that is, the lungs. From the minute it is born it will no longer be supplied with oxygen. It must start breathing through its lungs, and go on breathing through them until it dies, in the same way as its heart must go on beating until it dies. But for the new-born the heartbeat is less of a problem because it has had plenty of practice: its heart has been beating since three weeks after conception. Its lungs have had no practice at breathing air because there has been no air for them to breathe. Not only is the fetus floating in fluid—its lungs themselves are actually secreting fluid.

Exercising the muscles for raising and lowering the sternum (breast bone) in order to breathe is much more urgent than exercising the kicking muscles of the legs. Delay in activating the breathing muscles after birth could soon become fatal. If the brain is not continuously supplied with oxygen it will be damaged, and soon it will die.

So the fetus begins intermittently to rehearse breathing. It cannot breathe air, but it can go through the motions: it can expand its thoracic capacity. There used to be disagreement as to whether a mammalian fetus did or did not inhale amniotic fluid when it practised breathing movements, and whether it did or did not swallow amniotic fluid when it practised sucking movements. These questions can be answered by introducing a radio-opaque contrast medium into an animal's amniotic sac. It shows up later in the gastro-intestinal tract, but not in the lungs. So the fetus swallows the stuff it floats in, but does not breathe it in. Perhaps that is one reason why the lungs secrete their own fluid—to prevent inhaling. Swallowing bits of floating débris does no harm to the gut, but even the smallest particles could damage the lungs.

A far more unexpected discovery was made in 1975 by K. Boddy and G.S. Dawes, when it was demonstrated that in the case of fetal lambs—and there is no reason to assume it is not also true of humans—the 'breathing' episodes coincide with episodes of REM phenomena, that is, the Rapid Eye Movements seen in sleeping adults.

This is very odd indeed. It almost hints at the surreal proposition that the baby is prophetically dreaming that it has already been born and had better behave itself accordingly by pretending to inhale and exhale, while its eyes follow the restless movements of the imaginary people or creatures that populate its dreams.

However, a baby has never seen a rapidly moving object and is incapable of summoning up a mental image of one, just as the congenitally blind are. And it has been discovered in connection with adults that neither the fact of dreaming nor the quality of the dreams has any close correlation with rapid eye movements, as previously believed.

Perhaps the baby needs to exercise its eye muscles in the same way as it needs to exercise its breathing muscles, and parsimoniously practises them both together, during a rest period when the more strenuous kicking and stretching movements of its limbs are switched off. It could even be that our own REMs are merely a hangover from a prenatal behaviour pattern, and the very fact of sinking so deeply into slumber that all limb movements are inhibited is enough to trigger this little primal dance of the eyeballs.

Immediately after birth, a baby's preferred mode of breathing is not quite the same as our own. We can breathe either by raising the sternum or by depressing the diaphragm, or by any combination of the two. We seldom make a conscious choice unless we are singers or actors or athletes being professionally coached to think about our breathing. The baby makes its own decision. When it first starts breathing, its lungs are inflated exclusively by movements of the diaphragm. In fact, when it takes a really deep breath—perhaps in order to utter its first yell—the diaphragm goes down so far that the sternum is actually depressed instead of being raised.

This suggests that the diaphragm—which is one of the heftiest muscles in the whole body—must have been strengthened in advance of that yell by indulging in some kind of violent or strenuous activity. And so it has been: the activity is involuntary, and is called hiccuping.

Unborn mammals hiccup frequently. We also hiccup after we are born, but the incidence of these diaphragmatic spasms becomes increasingly rare, and older people may go for years without experiencing one. No one has been able to work out what purpose they serve. It could be that hiccups and REMs are both hangovers from an earlier stage of the life cycle. We are always ready to explain infantile features by reference to what the infants are destined to become; we are much less ready to explain apparently pointless features of our own physiology by reference to what we once were.

13

Birth

If all goes well the fetus will remain *in situ* for 38 weeks before its career as an endoparasite comes to a sudden end. By that time it will be (on average, according to World Health Organisation statistics) about 20 inches long and about seven-and-a-half pounds in weight. Full term males are slightly larger than full term females.

Not all the unborn are able to retain their tenancy for this length of time, or to attain these dimensions. Some embryos are malformed and spontaneously abort, often before the mother is aware she is pregnant: indeed, it is generally believed that only a minority of conceptions result in a live birth. Others are below average size or are born prematurely. Their development may have been affected if the mother's health is not good, or if she is in the habit of indulging in noxious substances such as alcohol, nicotine or other drugs.

The mother is also often warned that her baby's well-being may be affected by her state of mind. This advice is less helpful. Doubtless it is an excellent thing for a woman to remain happy and serene throughout the months of pregnancy, but these states of mind are not always obtainable at will; if they were, she would surely have taken steps to be happy and serene for her own sake, whether she were pregnant or not.

Particularly unhelpful are the hints sometimes given (hopefully, not by doctors) that difficulties in gestation or delivery are give-away signs that subconsciously she does not 'really want' the baby. Even apes may occasionally suffer from morning sickness, but they are spared the additional irritation of having it ascribed to obscure Freudian motives.

Everywhere in the world the most influential factor affecting the well-being of the mother and the child is poverty. In prosperous countries four per cent of babies are born prematurely. In poorer countries it is ten per cent. Within the developed countries, health problems associated with pregnancy and delivery are four times as common in low income groups as in the middle classes. By the WHO's birth-weight criterion, the United Kingdom has one of the poorest records in Europe.

However, evolution is the story of the survivors. The fetus whose development we have been following has now reached full term. It is in good health, and it will have a normal delivery. Even with these provisos, it is just about to embark on what has been called the worst journey in the world.

From time to time throughout the pregnancy there have been gentle, sporadic contractions of the uterus. Presumably in the mother's body as well as the child's, muscles which have seldom or never been flexed before need some trial runs to limber up for what lies ahead. But for the inmate cushioned in its water bed, these would be felt as nothing harsher than caresses.

Now they become more frequent, more regular and much more forceful. The formerly hospitable walls surrounding it contract in a strenuous effort to diminish the size of the uterine cavity and its contents. The contents, being non-compressible, are shoved downwards towards the neck of the womb, which initially bears no resemblance whatever to an exit. It has to be forced open; and the only available battering ram to bring this about is the baby's head. This is Stage One, and if it is a first baby the process continues for something between 13 and 24 hours, though the time usually shortens progressively with succeeding pregnancies. By the end of this time the baby's head has entered the neck of the womb and, if the amniotic sac has not ruptured before, it does so now, and the waters leak away.

This has the effect of causing the mother to increase the force being applied to the child's buttocks. The involuntary contractions of the uterus are now augmented by powerful contractions of the abdominal muscles. This is State Two. It can be a painful business for the mother, and it is impossible to believe that it is not painful for the baby also. The contractions are liable to be accompanied by kicking and spasmodic movements of its arms. The increased pressure on its buttocks is transmitted up its spinal column to the base of its skull, and this forces the head forward until the chin is touching the breastbone.

In this position it is propelled onwards until it encounters the bony pelvis, and the slope of the pelvic floor twists its head until it has rotated 90 per cent and is, as it were, looking over its shoulder. A little lower down, because its mother is a biped, it finds that the vagina has a kink in it, and it has to negotiate a 90 degree turn. The exigencies of this new hazard force its chin farther and farther away from its breastbone; its head is now bent backward as extremely as it was formerly bent forward, and it is leading with its chin. A little farther on, the angle of the head usually reverts to normal to facilitate a 'crown presentation'. The top of the head is propelled into the tight grip of the pubic ring.

The compression of its skull is only one of its problems. Throughout the hours of labour it has been intermittently deprived of oxygen, because each contraction compresses the placenta and the umbilical cord and temporarily cuts off its blood supply. It finds itself in a horrible and alarming predicament, and this leads to a surge in the production of catecholamines—the 'stress' hormones. In the infant during birth these hormones reach an even higher level than its mother is currently experiencing, higher in fact than in a person having a heart attack.

In adults, when the adrenalin glands are stimulated to produce stress hormones, they secrete adrenalin, and to a lesser extent noradrenalin, into the bloodstream to cause a 'fight or flight' reaction. The net effect is to accelerate the heart rate, dilate the bronchioles of the lungs to aid respiration, speed up the metabolism and shunt the blood away from organs such as skin, intestines and kidneys towards those that need to be active in emergencies—the heart, the brain and the skeletal muscles.

This would not be a particularly helpful response in the tight spot the fetus finds itself in. Both fight and flight are unavailable to it. So is deep breathing, since it has no air to breathe. No exertion of its skeletal muscles could serve any useful purpose, for it has no room to manoeuvre. The speeding up of its heart rate would only aggravate the recurrent shortage of oxygen, which is one of its main problems.

However, it has one thing going for it. The catecholamines surging through its veins in vast quantities are not being transmitted from its mother's bloodstream. By now it has gone into production on its own account and is producing a hormonal mixture tailored to its own requirements. In adults the secretion of the adrenal medulla contains 80 per cent adrenalin and 20 per cent noradrenalin— a compound similar in most respect but differing in its effect on the heart. In the fetus these proportions are reversed. Moreover, the supply is supplemented by additional adrenalin from specialised tissues surrounding the aorta. The main purpose of these is to enable it to survive birth, and they disappear in the course of childhood.

The preponderance of noradrenalin inhibits the flow of blood (and hence, of oxygen) to the skeletal muscles, and directs most of it to keeping the brain well supplied. At the same time the noradrenalin causes the heart rate to slow down instead of speeding up.

Hugo Lagercrantz and T. A. Slotkin have described how:
'The effect on the oxygen-deprived fetus mimics the diving
reaction seen in marine mammals: the blood flow to all
but the most vital organs is restricted, and the resulting
blood pressure increase enables the new-born to survive
the hazards of its journey, albeit with an oxygen debt akin
to that of a sprinter after a run.' Within 30 minutes of
delivery, the catecholamine level begins to decline, and
by two hours after birth has returned to normal resting
level.

Thus, in normal circumstances the system works well,
but under conditions of high-tech. obstetrics it may hit a
bit of a snag. In many hospitals it is standard practice for
the fetal heartbeat to be closely monitored, and if it
develops irregularities it is taken as a sign of fetal distress
calling for an emergency Caesarian section. It may well be
a correct diagnosis, in which case a life has been saved.
But the hormonal surges normal to the birth process may
show up on the monitors as danger signals. The prudent
surgeon—especially in the litigation-prone USA—dares
leave no stone unturned, and some years ago it was
reckoned that 50 per cent of the infants surgically delivered
turned out to show no clinical signs of asphyxia, and could
have been delivered normally.

Caesarians save many lives, but they entail some cost
to the baby, as well as to the mother. It has long been
recognised that breathing difficulties are commoner in
babies delivered by this method. The reason is that during
gestation liquid is naturally secreted into the lungs, and it
used to be assumed that during natural childbirth this
liquid was physically squeezed out by the compression
undergone in the course of delivery.

Apparently it is not that simple. It has been demonstrated in sheep that the surge of catecholamines—
whether naturally produced during delivery or artificially
administered—serves other purposes in addition to slowing down the heartbeat. It also causes the immediate cess-

ation of the secretion of lung liquid. The liquid is absorbed ready for the infant to commence air breathing, and there is increased production of a substance called surfactant which helps the alveoli (air passages) to remain open. In emergency Caesarians, where labour has begun, the surge has already been triggered and breathing is less affected, but in elective Caesarians planned in advance to by-pass labour, the lungs are liable to be waterlogged, and active measures have to be taken to ensure the transition to air-breathing when the baby emerges into the light of day.

There is some evidence to suggest that its distant ancestors more probably emerged into the dark of night. Many primates are designed to give birth at a particular time of day, and it is usually their normal resting period. Thus galagos, which are nocturnal, always give birth in the day-time, and many diurnal monkeys regularly give birth at night. Most primates are diurnal, and that is one reason why parturition of primates in the wild is seldom observed.

It is easy to see why night birth is adaptive for them, especially if they belong to a social species in which staying with the band is the best protection against predators. One macaque which, for some reason, broke the rule and gave birth by daylight, was seen in some distress whenever the band moved on, hurrying to catch up with her companions when the baby's head had just emerged and again after birth, but before the placenta had been delivered.

There seems to be no preferred period for the gorillas. Feeding gorillas do not need to move far or fast, and even if one becomes separated for a time, it is too big to be in much danger from predators. Human babies may be born at any time in the twenty-four hours, but there is an unmistakable remnant of an anti-daylight tendency. Statistics show that the likeliest time for delivery is between one and six in the morning.

Stage Two ends when the baby enters the world and takes its first breath.

After birth, many species of mammals in the wild are endowed with the instinct to sever the umbilical cord with their teeth. (In more than one observed birth of squirrel monkeys, this instinct has misfired, so that the mother has chewed for some time on her baby's tail before correcting her mistake.)

In most mammals, too, the separation of the baby from the cord is a simpler and neater process than in the case of humans. In animals like cats and dogs, for example, there is no navel on the lines of the human model. There is at most a small, smooth patch like an old vaccination mark, or like the leaf scars left on the stems of a deciduous plant when it sheds its leaves in winter. There seems no obvious reason why, in apes and ourselves, the cord drops away less readily and leaves a lifelong scar behind.

Besides severing the cord, another instinct common in female land mammals after parturition is eating the placenta (the afterbirth), possibly for its nutritive value, possibly lest the scent of it attract predators. This practice is found not only in carnivores, but also in herbivores who may eat nothing but grass throughout the rest of their lives. But in the higher primates, nothing about sex or parturition is as instinctive as it is in less advanced species. A captive gorilla who has never witnessed a birth has no inner voice telling her to eat the placenta any more than to bite through the cord. In fact, for the first half-hour, if it is her first-born, she seems to have very little idea of what she is to do with the baby. It has taken her by surprise. She may lick it and push it around on the floor of the cage for some time before it occurs to her to pick it up and then, as likely as not, she will hold it with its back to her, or upside-down, before she gets the hang of it.

Some of the mammalian instincts have also been lost to the human mother. Like the gorilla, she feels no irresistible impulse to bite the cord or to eat the afterbirth, though it is true that some women, having read that the placenta is full of valuable nutrients and trace elements, decide that they owe it to themselves and the baby to recycle it. Fried with onions, it is said to be very palatable.

However, anything the mother lacks in instinct is more than made up for by her greater understanding. When the baby is handed to her there is no danger that she will hold it the wrong way up or the wrong way round: she knows what is expected of her. She is experiencing her own hormonal surge, less massive than the baby's but more complex. There is no time of her life at which innate reactions are stronger, and it might be assumed that now, if ever, the emotions that 'Nature' has decreed for her will be in the ascendant. But there is also no time of her life at which she is more at the mercy of powerful human social conditioning. Everything in her experience has combined to impress upon her what she should be feeling now and how totally it depends on her situation in life: whether she should feel pride at having produced a beautiful baby, or shame at bringing another bastard into the world, or despair at having another mouth to feed.

Unlike the gorilla, she has not been taken by surprise. She has known for a long time what was going to happen. And suddenly there it is—small, outraged, squirming, streaked with blood, slathered with vernix, noisy, alive. One of us.

What kind of reception is it going to get?

14

The Wanted

There have always been some women for whom the greatest tragedy in their lives was that they longed for a child but could never have one. For others, the tragedy was that they had a baby in the wrong circumstances, or that they had too many of them. In those cases it was fertility rather than infertility that wrecked their lives. Throughout most of human history there was little that women could do in either predicament except petition gods or goddesses to answer their prayers.

In the present century scientific advances have enabled a minority to exercise more control over this aspect of their lives. But in some quarters the reaction to all of these developments—whether for suppressing fertility or promoting it—has been hostile.

The time-honoured way of producing a child is by inserting a penis into a vagina. In some societies in the past, a conventional religious upbringing meant that a definite yuck-factor was attached to this procedure. Celibacy was held to be the highest ideal but, for those who were not up to it, sex was permissible under prescribed conditions and for the purpose of reproduction. Somebody had to have children, otherwise even the supply of celibates would dry up.

But any revulsion towards the sex act has recently been dwarfed by the greater revulsion some people feel at the idea that babies might be conceived without it. Every step along this road has been met with demands that it be outlawed, and warnings that the spectre of Frankenstein was raising its ugly head.

After a while, the sense of shock tends to wear off. In vitro fertilisation, for example, now seems unlikely ever to be banned. It has brought too much happiness to too many people, and the children of parents who have gone to such lengths to give life to them patently have nothing 'unnatural' about them. They give no ammunition to those who say they should never have been born.

Controversy flared again with the first use of egg donation, and was recently inflamed by headlined reports of a baby born to a woman past the age of menopause, and a black woman giving birth to her husband's all-white baby. Some legislation with regard to these techniques may well be advisable if only because solemn legal matters can be involved, like the inheritance of property and titles. Complicated ethical issues are also said to arise. Was the black woman betraying her race by wanting a white baby? Is it ageist to deny a woman fulfilment because of her date of birth? Have the women who apply for IVF been brainwashed into imagining they want to start a family? Much of the agitation seems to be based on the apprehension that floodgates are being opened. What if everybody did it?

Everybody is not going to do it. For the 90 per cent with no fertility problem, the old fashioned way of baby-making is in no danger of losing its popularity. Very few people over fifty have any desire to spend the evening of their lives in the exhausting business of raising a child from scratch; of that small number only a small percentage can afford to try and, of that smaller number, only a small percentage would succeed.

Among younger women many have no desire for a child. Fortunately, nowadays most of them feel free to say so, and any pressures to make them feel apologetic about that decision should be resisted. But there remains, it is said, one person in a hundred who is 'affected by infertility': they want a child and their wish is not granted. The problem is commoner than it used to be, and no one is quite sure of the reason. When the tendency first became apparent, it was attributed to the behaviour of women. More women nowadays, it was pointed out, wish to get a foothold on a career before starting a family, and by the time they realise that their optimum breeding years will soon be over, their ability to conceive has lessened. Another suggestion was that since the Sixties they had become too promiscuous, that unsafe sex in the heyday of the Pill had led to a wider incidence of minor temporary venereal infections which left a legacy of infertility.

More recently, attention has been transferred to male infertility: there is said to have been a 50 per cent drop in the sperm count of the average male in the last fifty years. But this, too, was felt to be somehow, indirectly, caused by women. Too many of them were taking the Pill, and the oestrogen must in some way be leaking into the environment. Or else they must be feeding their baby boys with formula made from the milk of cows already in calf, and there must be oestrogen in it. (That was disproved.) The latest culprit to be fingered is neither men nor women, but the plastics industry which, in the last forty years, has released into the environment some 20,000 tons of a substance (nonylphenol) which is akin to oestrogen and tends to end up in the water supply.

Or, finally, there is a wild guess that sounds like science fiction or the work of Gaia: that is, that declining fertility signifies that overcrowding and overpopulation of the planet is triggering some kind of biological backlash, by analogy with the multiple diseases that attack our food plants when the 'monoculture' is carried too far. The only statistical support for this idea lies in the curious fact that in all hinterlands surrounding the world's great conurbations, when all other factors have been allowed for, the birth-rate rises with distance from the city centre, and the cities themselves are population 'sinks'. So when we read that Finnish men have sperm counts higher than the European average, it is hard to know whether it is because the air and water are cleaner up there, or because the people are thinner on the ground.

Among those who are affected by infertility, many come to terms with the situation, and either adopt or seek some other outlet for their energies. Others turn to the fertility clinics. The idea that they are driven to this by communal propaganda in favour of the nuclear family will not hold water. It is absurd to suppose that the women who spend thousands of pounds and wait for years and jump through all the hoops required to secure an IVF baby, with no guarantee of success, are doing it because they think it is the modish thing to do.

The desire to have a child is a natural appetite. It has obvious survival value, like the appetite for sex. It has well-attested primate roots—a childless chimpanzee may try to steal another's baby, or beg to be allowed to hold it for a while. In humans it is by no means universal, but it can be powerful, and now—for a lucky few—their desires can be fulfilled. It is admittedly unfair that the techniques are more readily available to the rich than to the poor: the world is an unfair place. But it would not be made better if we said of every new product or service: 'Until everybody can have this, nobody shall have it'.

But should they be trying so hard to have babies when there are too many people in the world already? The question is not so pertinent as it sounds. According to a recent survey, 50 per cent of the babies born are hoped for and welcomed; 25 per cent are unplanned but accepted with good grace; 25 per cent are unwanted. That means that if every woman got her wish, the birth-rate would drop by a quarter.

The upset caused by individual cases recently (1994) seems excessive. The black woman's white baby wasn't a harbinger of the blanching of the planet. Even if every mixed-marriage mother wanted a baby the colour of her husband, it would have no ultimate effect because half of the husbands would be black; and the number of people with colour prejudice who end up in mixed marriages must be vanishingly small.

The menopausal woman caused the greatest yuck-reaction, and it is true that there is a strong tendency to find older people yucky whatever they do. This one seems to have harmed nobody, and to have been attacked on ethically shaky grounds.

Apart from calling the process unnatural—it was no more unnatural than liposuction and breast implants—it was said to be unfair to the child because the mother might die. Any of us might do that. A woman over fifty has a slightly higher than average chance of traumatising her child by dying in the next fifteen years, and a slightly lower than average chance of doing it by divorcing in the next fifteen years.

Some said it would be cruelly embarrassing for the child when she reached, say Standard Three, because the mother fetching her child from school would be older than the others. Presumably, such a child would also be embarrassed if her mother were lame, or badly dressed, or fat, or had a funny accent. How stereotyped does a mum have to be? To protect all little girls from the taunts and jeers of their classmates we could arrange to have all non-stereotypic women sterilised, or ask them kindly to stay in the house where no one would see them. Or we could work out how to re-educate those brats in Standard Three.

There is, however, one category of women who should most certainly never have babies. It consists of the women who don't want them.

15

The Unwanted

In many species parental care does not have to be learned—it is hard-wired into their patterns of behaviour. Nesting birds are programmed with detailed instructions on how to build a nest, and how to respond to the stimulus of a nestling's gaping beak by stuffing food into it. It is the automatic nature of the response that makes some of them such easy dupes of the cuckoo.

In the higher primates parental care—which is almost exclusively maternal care—is partially learned behaviour. A female ape not infrequently loses her first-born through ineptitude, but gains expertise with practice. The infant, if it survives, is the core around which her existence revolves. It is the most interesting thing in her life. Apart from eating and sleeping, the baby is her chief source of physical gratification, as she is the baby's. It is a source of psychological satisfaction, too, because having a baby enhances her status in the group. Sex has lost all its appeal for her, and she has lost all her sexual attraction for the males in the group; she will not come on heat again until the infant is weaned. This provides her with a foolproof system of family planning, ensuring that there will never be more offspring than she can easily cope with at any one time.

In these circumstances, there can be no question of her not wanting the baby. In the first place, it conflicts with none of her needs and, in the second place, there is nothing else for her to want—no possessions she covets, no other life-style she can aspire to.

Our own babies are directly descended from infants who could command that kind of 100 per cent round-the-clock mothering. They behave as if they expect the same treatment, and in some human societies they still get something closely approaching it. Although they cannot—like young primates—cling to their mothers and support their own weight, they can be carried everywhere papoose-fashion or on the hip or in a sling or a shawl, in constant contact with the mother. In that kind of régime babies very seldom cry.

But although, in normal circumstances, young animals can depend on the tender loving care of their mothers, that does not mean their lives are never threatened by their own kind. In some species they are in danger from adult males—usually not their fathers. For example, a lion taking over a pride will usually kill any cubs sired by the male he has just ousted. This hastens the day when the mother will come into oestrus again and be ready to conceive cubs of his own.

Male bears are also in the habit of attacking cubs. Bears do not enter into any kind of consort relationship with females; it is not known whether a male in those circumstances can distinguish his own cubs from those of another. There may be some pheromonal distinction which he can detect by smelling them, or possibly he kills for the sport of it, or for food.

Sometimes, if they anticipate this kind of disaster, the mothers themselves will destroy their own brood. A child with a breeding pet rabbit or mouse may disturb the straw of the nest ever so gently to get a better view of the litter, only to find later that the smell of a stranger coming so close to them has spelt their doom.

Male rats will kill offspring not their own but, in that case, the females have evolved a mechanism which often precludes infanticide. If a pregnant female becomes aware early enough of the presence of a strange male rat, the embryos she carries will disappear. It does not require threatening behaviour on the part of the male, or even the sight of him, to bring this about. The smell of him wafted into the female's cage is enough to cause the development of the unborn to go into reverse, like a video tape run backwards. This mechanism has presumably evolved because the termination of the pregnancy is preferable to the birth of a litter which will not survive: better for the mother, and certainly no worse for the young.

In some species, the pheromonal embargo is enforced even earlier—not merely before delivery, but before conception. Cape hunting-dogs live a precarious existence. The pack may be able to find food enough for the raising of one litter in a season if all the members of the pack co-operate in helping to raise it, but if three or four litters were competing for the same scarce resources, it could be that none would survive. The presence and smell of the dominant female is enough to ensure that the other females never come on heat, and therefore never mate.

Somewhere along the evolutionary path which changed us into the kind of creatures we are today, some of the evolutionary safeguards which regulated reproduction in our predecessors have been lost.

One of these was oestrus. There is no periodicity in our sexual behaviour. Some researchers have contested this, reporting that there is in fact a slight increase in the sexual activity of females at and around the time of ovulation. Up to a point this could be restated by saying that there is a decrease in the sexual activity at and around the time of menstruation, which would be entirely understandable without postulating any cyclical variation in the libido.

If there is any residual vestige of a monthly peak in female sexual appetite it must be very slight indeed. On this issue perhaps the testimony of literature would carry as much weight as science. Throughout recorded history males have taken the liveliest interest in the sexual responses of females and have communicated to one another detailed accounts of their conquests. Some of them, claiming vast experience in such matters, have bequeathed helpful hints about the secrets of their success. But nowhere in the world has a belief in a lunar cycle of female accessibility become part of the traditional folk wisdom.

The loss of oestrus meant, among other things, that humans lost the most important of the natural controls guaranteeing that births would be spaced out, as they are in our nearest primate relatives. One of the provisions is still operative in our species, namely, the contraceptive effect of breast-feeding. In some tribes women who want to postpone their next pregnancy continue to suckle their latest child for three or four years. In developed societies, however, it is never continued that long, and sometimes is never embarked upon.

Another natural control is spontaneous abortion. Many early miscarriages are benign, in that they are not due to viral infection or anything wrong with the mother, but are a method of eliminating unfit embryos at an early stage.

One illustration of how this process operates was reported by James Neel and Alan Bittles to the American Association for the Advancement of Science in 1993. They had conducted extensive researches in a part of India where there was a strong tradition of marriage between cousins, and they had expected to find evidence that this practice leads to lowered standards of health in the general population due to in-breeding.

Instead, they discovered that conceptions in women who had married their cousins were twice as likely to end in spontaneous abortions as conceptions in women married to non-relatives (50 per cent compared with 25 per cent). As a result of this, the babies actually born were equally healthy in both groups.

People differ from animals in one important respect. For

good or ill, they can see into the future. They know that the baby at its mother's breast will need feeding not only now when food is free, but for many years to come. And they are sometimes in a situation where they calculate that one more would be one too many.

The earliest method of population control was infanticide. We have no way of knowing how often it happened among the scattered bands in Europe's Ice Ages, but there are peoples for whom infanticide was a recognised part of their culture to within living memory. It was found, for example, in the Arctic, where conditions were so harsh that hunger was always the chief threat to life, and on small remote Polynesian islands where conditions were at first so favourable that the population rapidly outgrew the resources and then, having burned their boats, had nowhere else to escape to.

Eskimos, before they came into contact with Western civilisation, lived permanently on the perilous edge of subsistence. When a boy was born he was given a name immediately, but a girl was not named until the matter of her survival had been weighed in the balance. The data suggest that half the female pregnancies were terminated at birth to make room for a male pregnancy. Yet the perils of hunting were such that the adult sex ratio was close to 50:50. If a baby was the third or fourth girl in the family, the decision would probably be taken to smother her or put her outside to freeze. Among the Netsilingmiut, it was often the grandmother who advised about what course of action would be best for the family. No one could accuse her of wantonly sacrificing a precious life for any selfish motive. As soon as she herself became more of a handicap than an asset to the family, she would certainly accept, and might propose, that next time the family moved on she would say goodbye and stay behind. It was not a matter of morality but of basic survival. The incidence of infanticide tended to vary with the extremity of the temperature, and since the Eskimos came under the provisions of the welfare state, infanticide among them is virtually unknown.

Every culture, including our own, deplores and discourages murder. But every culture, including our own, exempts some particular kind of killing, which it sanctions as being a regrettable necessity. Among the Inuit it is (or was) infanticide. In the developed countries it is war. We can hardly claim that ours is the superior form of morality. Dead babies are no less dead if their parents were also killed by the same bomb in the same patriotic cause.

In Europe, after the advent of civilisation, infanticide was not recognised or socially approved. It did not come to an end, but became furtive; throughout the Middle Ages there were dumps outside the cities to which unwanted babies were secretly taken by night and exposed to die. But by the nineteenth and early twentieth centuries it was increasingly giving place to abortion.

Richard Titmus pointed out that in England during the 1890s the average working-class woman experienced ten pregnancies and spent fifteen years in pregnancy and nursing. To maintain that average, for many those numbers must have been considerably exceeded. Many of the children died early, as any churchyard of the period illustrates. In cities and in the countryside, for the poorest women there was endless drudgery; the description of life as 'a vale of tears' was only too accurate.

For most of them there was no way out. The remedies available—'pills for female ailments'—were often priced out of their reach; it was hard enough to find money for food. Cheaper and more drastic remedies were less publicly on sale, such as potions made of herbs, gin and salts at ten pence a pint, or uglier concoctions laced with gunpowder or rat poison. We do not often hear the voices of the women driven to such straits, but a few comments are on record. One mother of fifteen children said: 'I'd rather swallow the whole chemist's shop and the man in it than have another kid.'

These were sometimes designated the undeserving poor. Their betters exhorted them to practise foresight, thrift, abstinence and continence. But, for the women, abstinence—or even *coitus interruptus*—was not theirs to command.

The other category of women often driven to despair consisted of the young and single. Chastity before marriage was the ideal, especially in the middle classes and the respectable Nonconformist working-classes. It was a sensible rule and, as long as everyone in the peer group subscribed to it, not difficult to observe. But, for those who slipped, the retribution was appalling. Revealing the pregnancy and keeping the baby could be the ultimate disaster. It meant automatically the loss of a job. Forty-six per cent of the illegitimate children in Britain in 1911 were born to women who had gone into domestic service. It meant a girl branded for life as a fornicator and a child branded for life as a bastard.

It could be argued that these women should have bowed to their fate. Many did, and survived—there were workhouses, there were orphanages, there were baby-farms and brothels. But when they were lonely and terrified and far from home, it sometimes ended in a desperate act in a public lavatory, or behind a hedge, and the burying of the evidence.

It was against this historical background that the campaign for family planning was launched. The people who supported it believed that contraception was better than infanticide and better than abortion. They ran slap into the yuck factor: What they proposed was unheard of. It was flying in the face of nature. Most decent people felt only revulsion at hearing such matters openly spoken of on public platforms by women without shame.

The fiercest opposition came from those who opposed birth control on moral or religious grounds. They took it as their axiom that whenever a penis entered a vagina— whether in an act of married love, adultery, rape or incest—then the sperm must continue on its way unhindered and be given a sporting chance to score. Any other course was unnatural, disgusting and sinful.

The struggle for the acceptance of the principle of birth control was long and hard, but in many countries it is virtually over. The initial shock/horror reaction is worth recalling for the light it throws on human nature, and how violently we react to anything new in connection with a natural function that is so old.

The controversy over abortion is on a different plane. The issues are far less clear-cut, but it is being fought out just as passionately, with the result that extremists of both factions tend to make untenable claims.

The extreme version of the pro-life lobby is that once an egg has been united with a sperm it is a human being; to deter the implantation of a fertilised ovum—even with a morning-after pill—is the slaughter of an innocent. It is murder. The extreme version of the pro-choice lobby is that anything inside a woman's body is a part of her as long as it remains inside her, and she has the right to do what she likes with it because nobody else is involved.

In the later stages of pregnancy two people are involved. A fetus in the last weeks is a sentient human being by any reasonable criterion, whether it is lying in a uterus or prematurely in a cot. In any decision about whether or not it is to be born, the interests of both mother and child have to be considered, and wherever abortion is legalised, it is the State's thankless task to fix on a stage at which it becomes intolerable and illegal. The more accessible it is in the early stages, the less likely that anyone in the later stages would ever wish to contemplate it.

At the opposite extreme, an embryo in its early stages is not a sentient human being, but a bundle of cells. It is a human being only in the same sense that an acorn is an oak tree. But reason is irrelevant here because, for those who believe otherwise, the issue hinges on faith.

The absolutists on both sides have one thing in common:

their views undergo a subtle transformation as soon as the baby is born. Not even the most ardent pro-choicer would argue for the right to kill a day-old child. The pro-life campaigners look on every baby carried home from the hospital alive as a victory and a happy ending. They do not calculate how many of the children who end up neglected, physically and sexually abused or battered to death, were born to mothers in wretched circumstances for whom the birth was the last straw. Among the rights they claim for it one is signally missing—the right to be born to a woman by whom it is wanted.

The opposing standpoints on abortion seem irreconcilable, and perhaps they never will be reconciled. The best hope is that one day they may become obsolete. Even among the denominations that most vigorously promoted it, the belief that family planning is sinful is losing ground. If, and when, methods of contraception become sufficiently effective and available, the unwanted will be synonymous with the unconceived.

16

The New-Born

When the baby first enters the world it has been subjected to a very alarming experience. Its heart—still much bigger than an adult's, relative to its body size—despite the moderating influence of the noradrenalin, is thumping hard and somewhat irregularly. Immediately after birth the pulse is racing at 180 beats a minute compared with around 72 in an adult. Ten minutes later it has slowed down to 170, but it may take between 15 minutes and an hour to settle down to a resting rate of 120–140.

The new-born has two primary needs: oxygen and warmth. Extrapolating from our own experience, we tend to imagine that the first of these is the more urgent. When water-birthing was first introduced, there was a tendency to fear that a baby delivered under water would drown unless snatched out of it within seconds. But in the first minutes he is, to all intents and purposes, breathing freely through his belly button. Oxygen-laden blood is still being delivered to him via the umbilicus, and any pressure points which might have been restricting supply while he was negotiating the birth canal were instantly relaxed once he was clear of the pelvic ring.

Those who have experienced both water-birthing and traditional deliveries often report their impression that the baby, as well as the mother, seems to find water-birthing a less stressful process. These things are hard to quantify. In women able to make the comparison, the probability is that the newer water-birthing method was used for a later baby, and subsequent deliveries tend, in any case, to be quicker and easier than the first.

But if it could be proved that babies did prefer the birthing pool, it would not be surprising. Two of the shock discoveries the new-born has to make about his world are that he has suddenly become a lot heavier—if he is lying on a bed, it presses up at him—and that it is cold. These perceptions can come to him a little less suddenly if he spends a brief transitional time in the weightless medium he is accustomed to, a medium, moreover, that is maintained at blood heat. A full-term infant has a temperature slightly higher than its mother's, around 98.8° F. There is an immediate drop of 3° in the first hour after birth; within two hours it may have dropped 5°, and the baby can do nothing about it. When he is older he will be able to shiver, but in the first weeks he has not even acquired that capacity.

Sometimes laying the new-born on its mother's breast, in contact with her skin, has a calming influence. He is wet and naked, she is smooth and warm, and this warmth is her first gift to him. Most students of biology are familiar with Harlow's experiments with baby monkeys, demonstrating that in a cage with a 'mother' made of wire from which he can suckle milk, and a 'mother' made of cloth which gives him nothing, the baby spends much more time on the cloth mother. It is interpreted as meaning that the baby wants something that looks and feels more like a real live mother.

Fewer students are familiar with the further Harlow experiment which demonstrated that if the wire mother, besides giving milk, also blows a gentle current of warm air, then the baby spends more time on that one than on the cloth mother though it bears much less resemblance to a monkey. That does not mean the baby monkey does not want a real mother, but it does mean that one of the major aspects of her that he responds to and appreciates is her temperature.

At one time it was obstetric practice to leave the baby naked for a while, maybe to weigh it at once, and then to clean it up before wrapping it in a nice clean blanket that might otherwise get soiled. Nowadays, wrapping it up is a priority.

Another priority is tying a ligature around the umbilicus before cutting it. Animals in the wild, of course, have nobody to perform this service. In some new-born mammals there is a smooth muscle sphincter that loops around the cord at the umbilical ring; this sphincter is tightened at birth to constrict the veins and arteries and cut off the flow of blood between mother and baby.

Humans do not possess this sphincter but, nevertheless, there would be no dire consequences if the cord was not tied. Temperature is a vital factor in this connection also. When the temperature of the cord drops after birth, that triggers a secretion in the umbilicus of a hormone (bradykinin) which acts as a powerful constrictor of the veins and arteries, and arrests the flow of blood.

One hazard that confronts the obstetrician if the baby is a boy is the possibility that while he is gently easing its passage into the world, his spectacles may be the target of a surprisingly vigorous jet of urine. The baby has had plenty of practice at performing this trick. During his last weeks in the uterus he has been swallowing as much as 750 ml of amniotic fluid every day, and urine is beginning to constitute an increasing percentage of the fluid he floats in, despite the fact that it is constantly recycled.

Shortly after birth, usually within the first ten hours, he has to perform a function he has not yet practised— evacuating his bowels.

On the very rare occasions when it has happened before birth, it is a danger signal, usually denoting a shortage of oxygen. Normally it first occurs within the first ten hours after birth, and may well take place before his first feed, which raises the question of how there comes to be anything to evacuate. But over the months he has been swallowing dead cells from the inside of his mouth and throat, and stray particles floating in the amniotic fluid—lanugo hairs and fragments of vernix—which, together with secretions of the liver and pancreas, have accumulated in his colon and formed a sticky, viscous, greenish-black mass known as meconium.

Getting rid of it is quite an achievement on his part because his intestinal walls are remarkably thin at birth, with hardly any muscular development. The main function of the muscles that will develop later is to propel solid food along the alimentary canal, and it will be a long time before he needs to do that. However, the muscles of the colon are slightly better equipped and their exercise gets easier with practice. Once he is drinking his mother's milk the evacuate changes from the colour of caviare to a rather attractive shade between saffron and scrambled egg.

Volumes have been written about the deep psychological hang-ups that sometimes get into the way of the free flow of love from a new mother to her child. They seldom mention the fastidiousness which may have been sedulously inculcated as a womanly virtue for the past two or three decades, and now has to be battled with. Sexual mentors in the more outspoken agony columns will point out that smelliness and messiness can be a turn-off for erotic love, and urge the offender to take steps to rectify the matter. These things are no great turn-on for maternal love, either, but in this case the offender can do nothing. Love, they say, conquers all. In this relationship, the incontinence of the loved one at both ends is one of the first hurdles it has to clear.

For primates in the wild it is much less of a chore than it is for us. A mother seems to be aware by some body-language signal when the child is about to take a leak, and holds it away from her body until it has finished. Arboreal monkeys are in the happy position of being able to let everything go, knowing that it will disappear out of their ken. The young of terrestrial monkeys and apes are far more developed at birth than ours are, able to move around and squat more or less from birth, whereas ours can only lie around and wait to be cleaned up.

For however many millions of years this difference has existed, it has not led to any greater power of continence in our own species than in those of our primate relatives. It is sometimes assumed that these animals cannot be house-trained, but that is mainly because people rarely expend as much time and patience on educating an ape as we do on our own children.

In the 1930s W.N. and L.A. Kellogg adopted a young chimpanzee, Gua, at the age of seven-and-a-half months and treated him in the same way as their son Donald who was then a couple of months older. Both chimp and child learned to wee into a commode within about six weeks of the start of their training.

The Kelloggs record that, unlike Donald, Gua seemed from the beginning to have some kind of instinct that if she was sitting on someone's lap when she felt the urge to defecate, 'she *knew* she had to get down'. It might not have been instinctive; they speculate that her mother who raised her from birth may have taught her that by holding her at arm's length or pushing her away. Donald and Gua reached the same age (about 13 months) before being able to indicate in advance that they 'wanted to go'. In this connection Gua scored lower in only one respect: her emotions were more overpowering, and when frightened she was more likely to lose control of bladder or bowels or both.

The physical characteristics of a human child in his first year can be divided into three classes: those which are hangovers of features that were adapted *in utero*; those which are adaptive in the current stage of his life; and those which are peculiarly and enigmatically human.

An example of the first type is the shortness of his legs and the way he holds them, with the knees spread apart and bent, so that the soles of the feet face towards each other. In the confined space of the uterus that was a neat solution to a difficult packaging problem. But even after birth the infant at first positively resists any effort to straighten out its legs, even though it has now plenty of room to stretch. However, from birth onwards the legs grow rapidly in comparison with the rest of the body, and by puberty humans are unique among the apes in having legs that are longer than their arms.

In the days when rickets was common among poor children, inexperienced parents often feared from its appearance that their new-born was destined to be bandy-legged. But that appearance is an illusion created partly by the angle at which the legs are held, and partly by the distribution of the fat layer. In fact, a child's femur, like its spine, is straighter in the first year of life than it will ever be again.

Similarly, all babies appear flat footed. But an X-ray would show that the arch of a baby's foot is higher than in an adult, and the sole is flat only because of the accumulation beneath it of a deposit of fat known as the plantar pad.

The baby's general feebleness compared with primates of a similar age is also a hangover from the fetal environment, and is carried on into its period of independent existence because of the relatively immature stage of its development.

The most important adaptation to its current needs is the same as that of any other young mammal—locating a nipple and sucking. Most young mammals are guided in this quest by their sense of smell, and women still retain in the nipple and the areola surrounding it a concentration of the kind of apocrine glands which produce pheromones of which the baby may be conscious. But the sense of smell in humans of all ages is radically reduced. The chief sign of seeking behaviour in a new-born is that any touch on its cheek will cause it to turn its head towards that side, as if towards the breast.

Once its mouth contacts the nipple, it knows exactly what to do. The muscles of its tongue and around its mouth are in a more advanced stage of development than those in almost any other part of the body. Its tongue presses the nipple against the roof of its mouth—the palate. This is made easier by the fact that the palate of a baby is flatter than ours. To help it to prevent the nipple from sliding out, it has evolved a series of transverse ridges along the palate which have reminded some people of that tidal phenomenon described by Coleridge as 'the ribb'd sea sand'. The ridges have no further function in adult life and, like hiccups, become less in evidence as the years go by.

Some of the mysterious un-ape-like characteristics acquired before birth remain unchanged. The coat of body hair it shed *in utero* is not replaced, and only on its scalp does the hair grow longer. The all-over layer of fat is not only retained but continues to increase month after month, and does not reach its peak until the child is one year old.

On the other hand, the active sebaceous glands (which secreted the vernix caseosa) now enter a long period of latency. Only at puberty will they suddenly burst into action again in a big way, to the potential distress of acne-ridden teenagers.

In the course of its first year also the infant adds three more to its list of anomalous characteristics. The first is the massive growth in the size of its skull. In all other mammals the rate of brain-size increase slows down considerably at birth. In a human baby—because it is in a real sense 'an extra-uterine embryo'—the rapid fetal rate of brain size increase continues unchecked. The brain, like the legs, grows much faster than the rest of the body after birth. Within the first year of life (the 'extra-uterine' stage) it almost triples in size, from an average of 350 gms at birth to an average of 1,000 gms twelve months later. The other two anomalous developments arising in the first year are also unique to our species, but are more mystifying. Most people take it for granted that a bigger brain must be an asset to any animal that succeeds in acquiring it. But it is much harder to imagine why one particular branch of the ape family should acquire the capacity to weep. It is not a capacity we are born with. Charles Darwin observed that 'infants whilst young do not shed tears or weep, as is well known to nurses and medical men.'

Darwin devoted a great deal of attention to this problem. He observed that eye-watering in response to a physical irritation of the surface of the eye was quite different in its operation from emotional weeping. He first noticed this when he accidentally brushed the open eye of his eleven-week-old child with the cuff of his coat; the baby screamed and the affected eye watered copiously—but the other eye remained dry. Darwin made enquiries about the age at which emotional 'free weeping' first occurred—that is, tears running down the cheeks—and he discovered that it varied widely, from 42 days in one case to more than 110 in another.

His explanation was that the lacrimal glands require practice before they can operate. This was, he said, all the more likely with a habit like weeping, which must have been acquired since the period when man branched off from the common progenitor of the genus *Homo* and the non-weeping anthropomorphous apes. Another possibility is that the late onset of weeping, like the late onset of shivering, is connected with the human baby's entry into the world at an unusually early stage of development. It is conceivable that Lucy's babies could both shiver and weep from the time they were born.

Weeping, though a puzzling behaviour-pattern, is at least not deleterious. This is less true of the other physical change occurring in the first year of life—the descent of the larynx. In all land mammals, except humans, the top end of the windpipe (the larynx) is in contact with the back of the palate, so that air inhaled by the nostrils has its own exclusive pathway all the way down to the lungs. Our babies are born with this arrangement intact. But early in infancy—at some time between four and six months old—the larynx begins to move down to a position below the back of the tongue. This means that in older children and adults, the two openings leading to the stomach and to the lungs lie side by side low down in the throat. That is why it is so easy for food and drink to 'go down the wrong way'.

Evolutionists have occasionally been attacked for being so ready to describe any feature of any living thing as being adaptive—as if they were subscribing to the principle that 'whatever is, is good'. But the descended larynx is one phenomenon that has most stubbornly resisted all attempts to put a good gloss on it. Darwin deplored it as a thoroughly bad idea. Victor Negus, the greatest ever authority on the subject, denounced it in similar terms. Edmund Crelin, author of the standard reference book on the anatomy of the new-born, describes what happens, and adds the comment: 'Compared to the anatomy of the newborn infant, this is an undesirable arrangement'.

It was Crelin who first suggested a connection between the descent of the larynx and SIDS (Sudden Infant Death Syndrome—cot deaths). SIDS is found only in humans. Ninety per cent of these deaths occur before the age of six months, almost all of them during the period when the larynx has lost its connection with the palate and has not yet reached its final position low in the throat.

A new-born baby intensely dislikes breathing through its mouth. If its nose is blocked, it will make violent efforts to restore nose breathing, and only resort to breathing through its mouth when in danger of asphyxiation. Between four and six months, if for any reason (such as a slight cold) it had difficulty in breathing, it would struggle to restore nose breathing, but if it was lying at the wrong angle, the partially descended larynx could get into a position where the uvula could enter it and block it.

Face down is the wrong position. At one time it used
to be recommended, on the grounds that babies lying on
their backs might die through inhaling their own vomit.
In 1987 in the Netherlands a campaign was conducted
reversing this advice and counselling mothers to put the
babies to sleep on their backs or on their sides, but never
face down. A 40 per cent decrease in cot deaths throughout the country followed within twelve months. Similar
results followed a similar campaign in New Zealand.
No other advice on SIDS obtains such drastic results.
Studies have been made linking SIDS to various other factors such as low temperature or poor ventilation or infection, because the incidence is higher in winter. But while
these factors may be in some cases the precipitating cause,
the proximate cause has to be something to do with the
force of gravity. Otherwise, the position in which the baby
lies could not affect the outcome so radically. And the
only thing in the respiratory canal which is sufficiently
unattached to respond so freely to the force of gravity—
and is present exclusively in that particular age group—is
the loose end of the baby's windpipe, the semi-descended
larynx.

17

Interacting

The previous chapter, in the manner of earlier passages describing the fetus, was largely concerned with how the baby is physically constructed. But from the moment of birth, that is only part of the story. The heart-stopping thing about the new-born is that, from minute one, there is somebody there. Anyone who bends over the cot and gazes at it is being gazed back at.

From this point on, it would be dehumanising to continue to describe the baby as 'it'. There is no singular pronoun in English to describe a human being of indeterminate sex and that is unfortunate, because as far as our extra-uterine embryo is concerned, gender is meaningless to it. It faces a sufficiently daunting challenge in trying to recognise its basic membership of a species as complex as ours. Any attempt to identify with a subsection of it can be deferred to a later date.

But the matter is of primary importance to its parents and the rest of society. The chances are that, at the actual moment of birth, those in attendance had their eyes drawn as if by magnets to that portion of the anatomy which would enable them to use the correct grammatical protocol: 'he' or 'she'. That first glance sets up in their minds a wide and subtle web of expectations about how the child should behave and how they should treat it; what praises should be lavished on it (she's sweetly pretty, he's so strong and venturesome) and what terms of implied reproach (tomboy, crybaby) to steer it along the path society prescribes. The choice of one sex or the other for our narrative has to be arbitrary, but the arbitrariness of it is precisely part of the human predicament. The baby we are talking about is a boy. (The decision is a matter of convenience, not sexism. Mother and baby will be closely interacting for some time to come, and if each of them was a 'she' it would make it more difficult for the writer to juggle the pronouns.)

Taking the best-case scenario, he was born at full-term, he was a wanted baby, everything went smoothly, he is lying in her arms, she is smiling at him, and he can see her face. He is capable of turning his head to and fro and moving his eyes and he can suck and cry. But from the neck down he is almost totally disabled. He can jerk his limbs spasmodically, but he has as yet no more control over their movements than if he was suffering from severe cerebral palsy. He cannot speak or sit up; even if his torso is held upright he cannot prevent his head from wobbling.

An adult with anywhere near that degree of handicap soon makes the tragic discovery that most people tend to equate locomotor impairment with mental impairment. In the case of babies, mothers used to be told by the experts that, though the child might appear to be looking, he could not actually see anything. He might appear to be smiling, but it was only wind. For hundreds of years doctors promoted an even more distancing assumption—that babies could not feel pain. Circumcisions could be carried out without anaesthetic on the grounds that it doesn't really hurt them—they are not like us. People used to say the same about savages.

He can see and feel. He can register the good sensations that he is warm and comfortable and perhaps drinking warm milk. In association with these good feelings, and more or less filling his field of vision, we now know that he can see his mother's face. Part of our knowledge comes as a feedback from the study and treatment of adult handicaps. Quadruplegics—who can control no movements from the neck down—can operate buttons and switches by a device held in the mouth. Now, babies have been offered a somewhat similar method of communicating their preferences. Experiments have been set up arranging that, when they suck on a dummy, one of a succession of images is summoned up on a screen in front of them. The dummy is monitored so that the strength and duration of the sucking is known: the babies work harder to retain the pictures that appeal to them. The results tend to confirm deductions that were made by the earlier low-tech. method of offering them two pictures to look at and comparing the length of time they spent looking at each of them.

Given a choice of patterns, they prefer from the beginning those that somewhat resemble a face. Later they can distinguish a real human face from a drawing of one; later still they can distinguish that of their mother (or principal carer) from that of any other.

More remarkably, they can see what the face is doing, and from the first day of life are able to try to imitate it. This is a thing that not even mothers knew until scientists demonstrated it. If a mother makes faces at a baby a day or two old, she may be rewarded by seeing that she is holding his attention, because babies find moving objects more interesting than immobile ones. But it will not be at all obvious that he is copying her, because the copying is not instantaneous. He is an absolute beginner. By the time he has worked out what to do with his muscles to make his tongue stick out as hers is doing, she may have moved on to something else—opening her mouth wide, or grinning.

However, if the 'tongue-out' or the 'open-mouth' expression is held long enough for him to register it and react, he is capable of copying it. These responses have been monitored carefully enough to prove they are not random. He cannot know what he looks like; he is not yet conscious of himself as being a separate person like the other people he sees around him, so the imitation must be as instinctive as sucking. In fact, although we use the word 'ape' to mean 'imitate', human children of all ages are more expert imitators than other primates are.

Apart from instinctive reactions, he is also beginning to use his brain, and he is using it for precisely the same ends as we would be using ours if we were in his predicament. He is trying to compensate for his multiple physical handicaps by seeking ways of gaining some power over his environment through understanding it better.

No one has quite worked out why the evolution of greater intelligence constituted a selective advantage for the earliest humans. It is a question seldom debated, because it is one of those matters on which we tend to take up a Jeffersonian stance: we hold this truth to be self-evident, that it pays to be brainy, and we have by now constructed a complex technological society in which there is a lot of truth in the proposition.

But animals in general tend to evolve no more intelligence than they need, in the same way as they evolve no greater speed or size, no larger ears or stronger talons than they need. It is by no means self-evident that one species of African primate would gain dramatically greater benefit from increased intelligence than other African primates. Brains are an expensive investment: the same amount of metabolic energy devoted to increased brawn might have paid equal or better dividends. If two specimens of *Homo habilis* (or even *Homo sapiens*) confronted one another naked on an African plain, it is no foregone conclusion that the small intelligent one would prove fitter to survive than the larger, less intelligent one.

The tacit assumption, as so often, is that the brain became more active in adults, to improve the chances of adult survival, although the problems faced by the earliest adult humans were not radically different from the problems faced by their primate cousins.

On the other hand, the problems faced by their infant offspring—once they began to be ejected at earlier and earlier stages of development—were unique. No other infant mammal is, as the scientists describe it, secondarily altricial.

The typical primarily altricial infant is one of a bunch of siblings. They are born with their eyes closed; even when they open them, there is nothing much to see because they have usually been hidden in a dark place. Between the times when their mother visits and feeds them, they huddle together, keep each other warm, and sleep, and grow. They do not use their intelligence because there is nothing for them to exercise it on. Later, by the time they emerge into the light, they are able to run about, tumble over each other and, if they see anything that interests them, go over to it and investigate it.

Our secondarily altricial baby has his eyes open. He can see things and recognise them at a stage of his development at which any monkey or ape would still be in the womb with nothing to look at or think about.

This state of affairs will continue not for a week or two, but month after month. He has no way of knowing what we know: that his disabilities are temporary. He begins his life in the bustling outside world as a functional quadruplegic; this is the kind of animal he is, and he sets about making the most of it. Between suckling and sleeping there is nothing much he can do to this end except lie and look and listen and try to put two and two together.

If he sees his hand moving in front of him, his eyes follow it. If, by chance, he flexes certain muscles the hand moves, and he finds this happens not once but every time. He discovers that his hand is one of the things that is always around and he can make it do things. He sees a face in front of him and learns to put it into a different category. It is not always around; he can make it do things, but only up to a point. If he smiles it will often, but not every time, smile back at him. If it has gone away and he cries, it will often—but not every time—reappear. The most important thing in his life is to increase his power of influencing this phenomenon. It is his lifeline, his food bringer, his locomotor organ, his enabler. Its catalytic powers are amazing. He can levitate when he desires to— he can rise up into the air, as all of us can still do in our dreams. But he can only pull off this trick in the presence of a human face—either this one, or another. That is the part of his universe that he most urgently needs to understand.

All primates can communicate their emotions and intentions to one another by visual signals, and so do we. But compared with other species we make far greater use of eye contact and facial expressions for this purpose. Monkeys and apes have a finite set of stereotypical facial expressions, in the same way as they have a finite set of vocal utterances: the expressions and the utterances are both involuntary. 'In comparison with man,' as Darwin pointed out, 'their faces are inexpressive.' Ours are so expressive that in trying to read other people's minds we concentrate almost exclusively on their eyes and faces— so much so, that when some years ago we were reminded that hands and feet and posture also betray our states of mind, this concept of 'body' language had something of the force of a revelation.

The same is not true of apes, and it seems likely that the difference arises in infancy. As Suzanne Chevalier-Skolnikoff observed, 'A striking difference between apes and humans . . . is the human incorporation of eye contact and the smile into the socialisation process. Whereas apes, like macaques, appear to become attached to the mother through tactile/kinaesthetic and possibly olfactory modes, by the beginning of the second month, the smile is a major part of the infant's attachment process.'

He is the only mammal that can maintain eye contact while he is suckling. The monkey or chimp baby gripping his mother's fur has his face clamped to her chest, and his mother's typical posture is gazing over his head into the distance.

It is on the basis of these handicaps and these assets that babies have to work out ways of controlling their mothers. 'Control' may seem an inappropriate word to describe the activities of such small and helpless creatures, but it will seem less inappropriate to those who have had intimate dealings with them. The first men to attempt a sociological survey of infant development prepared a list of questions to address to Scottish mothers; one of these was, 'How much time in a day do you spend nursing your baby?' The researchers were male, and they expressed a naïve astonishment at the frequent and heartfelt reply, 'A lot more than I want to, I can tell you that!'

The infant's strategy consists of a stick-and-carrot approach. His smiles and his laughter are rewards for his mother when she is behaving well; they are uniquely human. The smiles come very early, within days of birth. Laughter comes later, at an age which varies between individual children. One study recorded four children in the sample laughing at twelve weeks old, and one not laughing until the age of fifty-two weeks.

However, this was under laboratory conditions. The mothers themselves insisted, plausibly enough, that their children laughed at earlier ages when they were at home. They also protested that when urged by a researcher to make their babies laugh, they felt silly and couldn't put their hearts into it. That is not surprising. Viewed with a cold eye, feminine responses to babies can sometimes cause, as Dorothy Parker pointed out in one of her short stories, 'vicarious embarrassment'. She describes the behaviour of one trained children's nurse through the eyes of an unsympathetic employer.

'She would bring her long head down to Diane's tiny, stern face and toss it back again high on her rangy neck, all the while that strange words, in a strange high voice, came from her. "Well, her wuzza booful dirl. Ess, her

wuzza. Her wuzza, wuzza, wuzza. Ess, her *wuzz.*"'
Yet scientists themselves would now say that Parker's
Miss Wilmarth, whether by instinct or following an age-
old tradition, had got it dead right. The strange high voice,
the face appearing and disappearing, the repetitive syl-
lables, were all beautifully calculated to interest a new
baby and give its mind something to work on. And when
a mother behaves like that she is *not* performing for a
cold-eyed audience. However the rest of the world may
rate her charms, for the baby the face that comes and goes
in his daily life is the most fascinating sight in the world.
However, if left to its own devices, this fascinating sight
will appear too infrequently and disappear too soon for
the baby's peace of mind. Experience soon teaches him
that this state of affairs can sometimes be ameliorated by
uttering a loud noise. Human babies are the noisiest of all
young primates, not necessarily in the volume of the
sounds they utter, but in their duration. The Kelloggs noted
that if the baby chimp Gua hurt herself she would utter a
cry of pain and then shut up. If their son Donald hurt
himself, he would start to cry and go on crying. Protesting
cries from primate infants are invariably addressed to their
mothers. Even young baboons, who are habitually among
the most silent of young monkeys (sensible behaviour in
a predator-ridden environment) will often throw a noisy
tantrum at weaning time when they are pushed away from
the teat. There has now been extensive research into the
behaviour of young apes reared by human surrogate
parents. There are very many accounts of the young adop-
tees registering vocal protests at being physically separated from their minder, protests that can escalate into loud
displays of frantic frustration and despair in which they
hurl themselves to the ground and scream themselves
hoarse. But if, and when, they win their objective and are
picked up, the noise ends. It is the baby in its mother's
arms and *still yelling* that is the human speciality.
Presumably, this behaviour at some stage of human

evolution was of advantage to the baby, and presumably it is related in some way to its prolonged period of helplessness. If a young ape or monkey wants to stay near its mother it can cling to her fur and sustain its own weight—in the great majority of cases, from birth. If she moves away, it can follow her. In terrestrial species when it grows too big to cling and be carried under her belly, it can ride on her back. These strategies require a well-developed infant, and a mother with fur, and a horizontal back. In the human species these requisites are absent. Consequently, there has always been much more incentive for human mothers, as compared with other anthropoids, to put the baby down while she gets on with whatever she has to do.

In the case of early hominids, what she had to do would be foraging, an absorbing and necessary task which might well involve wandering some distance away. A baby's fitness to survive in those circumstances might well be related to the tirelessness with which he could keep on crying, to remind her that he was there and pin-point his location if she was in any doubt about it. It might have been then that our babies first evolved the kind of crying in which the on-button works more efficiently than the off-button.

Unfortunately, this adaptation has become counterproductive in modern conditions, sometimes dangerously so. In the open air the crying may have been a serviceable signal. But for a young mother or a young couple living in a bed/sit with an unplanned baby it can quickly become maddening. Sometimes a girl from a loveless background will go ahead with an unplanned pregnancy believing that at last there will be someone in the world who is hers alone and will love her unconditionally, and sometimes it works out well. But if she is young and inexperienced it can be hard to interpret that noise as love, when it goes on and on. Fewer babies would be battered if they would only keep quiet.

It is a truth universally acknowledged that all babies love their mothers, or those who function as their mothers. They do love them. But, as William Blake has told us, there are two kinds of love. There is the devouring kind in which:

> Love seeketh only self to please,
> To bind another to its delight.

The infant is an absolute beginner, greedy for life. Inevitably he seeks to bind. And ideally, in a parent/infant symbiosis, that baby love should lock into its counterpart, the mature and caring kind, in which:

> Love seeketh not itself to please
> Nor for itself hath any care
> But for another gives its ease
> And builds a heaven in Hell's despair.

But for fallible humanity in today's world, that is a very tall order.

18

Parenting

Campaigns for social reform are commonly based on the proposition that most of the inequalities in human life are artificially imposed. Societies based on slavery, on a caste system, or on race or class distinctions depend on the assertion by one set of people that they are innately superior to another set of people. These assertions have no basis in fact; they are ultimately based on the historical use of force to acquire powers that have over time become traditional and institutionalised. In many instances the assertion of superiority comes to be accepted even by those who are oppressed by it: they teach their own children to regard themselves as naturally inferior. But, however long such systems last, it is possible to eradicate them.

Differences of status between men and women were institutionalised by the same methods, and justified by the same arbitrary assertions of superiority. As with other hierarchical systems, the ruling sector buttressed its claims by exercising a near-monopoly of the rights to education and the ownership of property. The subordinate sector in general believed the claims and brought up its daughters to internalise that view of themselves.

There is one difference. The unequal division of labour between master and slave, between feudal lord and peasant, was made by humans. But the unequal distribution between males and females of the burden of bearing and raising the young was not a human invention: it existed long before the human race appeared. It can be reassessed and redistributed, but it cannot be lightly tossed overboard because it is part of the stuff we are made of.

The rule that the female provides the parental care is not universal in nature. In fish, for example, only about one in three species provides parental care of any kind, but among those who do, in half the cases it is the father who does the caring. He may guard the eggs, ventilate them with his fins, and/or when the eggs hatch brood the young in his mouth. In some amphibians, too, rearing the young is a paternal duty.

So what decides whether the male or the female takes on the responsibility? According to Richard Dawkins it depends on which parent can make the quickest getaway. In those species in which the eggs are laid slightly before the male covers them with sperm, there is a short time when the female can desert them and the male cannot; so she promptly makes her excuses and leaves. In mammals the opposite is true; there is a long period during which the male can desert his offspring but the female cannot because they are inside her.

In mammals, therefore, since fertilisation is internal, paternal care tends to be perfunctory or absent. Males, however, are prepared (indeed, by natural selection they are compelled) to provide paternal input into the rearing of the young if it would otherwise be so onerous that their offspring would not be successfully reared at all. Examples are birds, which may have a strictly limited period in which to rear their brood before the time comes to migrate. It can take two adults all the hours God sends to cram enough food into those gaping mouths.

The anthropoid apes lead a more leisurely existence and show no signs of possessing a paternal instinct. The dominant male in a group usually behaves tolerantly to the young and provides the juvenile males with a role model. He may allow them to take liberties with him when they are small and venturesome, teach them manners when they get older, and intervene to restore peace if the big ones are tormenting smaller ones. But he appears to do this in his role as their leader rather than as their father: in a large troop it is unlikely that a single male sired all the offspring, but the alpha male makes no distinction between them.

According to the general rule that males make the greatest contributions when the task of rearing is most arduous, we would expect the human male to have acquired some paternal behaviour patterns in the course of several million years, because the task of rearing the long-helpless, slow-growing human child is as arduous as they come.

This expectation is fulfilled. *Homo sapiens* males do display parental behaviour, and contribute a paternal input to a greater degree than any other primate. In most cultures a man will help to provide a nest to shelter the transmitters of his name and his genes, whether that input involves building a grass hut or working to pay a mortgage, and he will make a contribution to the feeding of his mate and her children.

But in all cultures also he appears to retain one anthropoid conviction: that young babies are things that females have, and that the hands-on care of them is a female responsibility.

There is a stage in the development of the young at which a father may spontaneously sit up and take notice of them, play games with them, prescribe his own rules about how he thinks they should behave. Once the young have passed that invisible threshold males play an important part in their education, but the Jesuit who asked to be given charge of a child's mind until it was seven years old would probably have been taken aback if a week-old child had been put into his arms. At that stage what goes on in its mind is not considered to be education.

So, throughout history, it has generally been taken for granted that rearing infants is women's work. But recently, women—who have taken to questioning so many of the eternal verities of social life—have questioned this one also. True, for nine months a woman is caught in the mammalian trap and cannot walk away from a baby which is inside her, but some of them fail to see why after it is born the care of it has to be their sole responsibility.

There is ample evidence that a woman is indeed biologically programmed to look after babies. Sixty million years of mammalian evolution have served to perfect the dovetailing of the infant's needs with the female capacity to satisfy them. A woman's milk is designed to give simultaneously ideal nourishment and some degree of protection against disease; it is always sterile and at the right temperature, and the composition of it changes over the weeks and months as the baby's requirements change. She secretes female hormones in increased quantities during and after pregnancy—mind-changing chemicals designed to make her behave less aggressively, more cooperatively, more unselfishly. It cannot be doubted that physically she is miraculously well adapted to the functions of baby-making and baby-rearing.

But, like the human male, she is not merely a mammal. She belongs to the same special subdivision of the mammals: she, too, is an anthropoid. That means that many of the stereotyped behaviour patterns which are instinctive and automatic in the lower orders of mammals are not instinctive and automatic in her: they have to be learned. In apes and monkeys, the classes of behaviour that have to be learned include not only clearly 'cultural' habits—like choosing which foods are good to eat, and how to use a stone to crack open a nut—they also include behaviours we tend to think of as instinctive, such as how to copulate, and how to deal with a baby.

If our knowledge of ape and monkey behaviour had been derived solely from studying them in the wild, it would have taken us longer to become aware of these surprising facts. Primates are social creatures. From the time they are born they see their elders mating and see the females nursing babies. The juvenile males indulge in pretend-mating, homosexual or heterosexual, practising mounting and pelvic thrusts long before they are old enough to ejaculate. The young females pester new mothers for the privilege of touching or holding an infant, or carrying it around under the supervisory eye of its mother.

By the time her first baby arrives a female ape in the wild may still be awkward in holding it or remiss in keeping it out of danger. But she already has a good idea of how it should be done, she has observed that motherhood conveys prestige, and if she makes mistakes there are older females around to put her right. Observing primates in groups in their natural habitat would not have revealed how deeply they are indebted to social conditioning for their sexual and maternal competence.

It is a very different matter with captive animals in zoos and laboratories. A male rhesus monkey that has been reared in isolation from birth may never succeed in mating. And a female that has been reared in isolation and then been mated has no idea what to do when a slippery little thing like a drowned kitten on a string emerges from her body. She is likely to push it away from her and retreat to a corner of the cage. Notwithstanding the surge of female hormones and the sixty million years of mammalian evolution, it does not 'come naturally' to her to devote herself to the new arrival. She has the biological potential to do so, but the potential is only realised in the right context.

Humans are more intelligent than rhesus monkeys, and to that extent their responses to the basic biological life-events are even less hard-wired. If a woman declares that it does not come naturally to her to love babies and want to mother them, she is telling the truth. If another woman declares that she longs passionately to have a baby and bring it up, she is telling the truth. Neither has the right to conclude that the other is being in the one case unnatural or, in the other case, hypocritically conformist.

In the most primitive societies it is virtually unknown for a woman not to want babies, probably because the social context is closer to that of primates in the wild. Mothers have higher status than childless females and lead more interesting lives. Babies are part of the communal life, and their feeding and their rearing are observed by other children from the time they are born.

In the more developed societies several things have conspired to destroy that state of affairs. One is simply greater affluence—access to the possession of a much wider range of artefacts and services, and a more gracious style of living. Babies are not conducive to gracious living, being noisy, messy, vulgar and unpredictable. They are no respecters of artefacts. Children are an expensive item, competition for the deployment of that well-known scarce resource—money. Other things being equal, mothers are less affluent, enjoy less prestige, and lead more isolated, less interesting lives than their contemporaries pursuing careers.

Another thing that has happened is the relegation of babies to ghettos. True, they are not herded together in one place. This ghetto is splintered into thousands of individual homes. In a survey conducted by Sheila Kitzinger, 38 per cent of the mothers questioned were alone with their babies for between eight and twelve hours every weekday. Once a baby is taken outside the home it is subjected to fairly strict conventions of apartheid. The mother/infant dyad (as scientists call it when talking about other species) is not admitted into workplaces, not welcomed in public buildings, hotels, pubs and theatres; is seldom encountered by non-parents anywhere except in supermarkets.

Young children, like some other animals and minorities, are allowed reservations in which to roam freely—playgrounds or public parks—but, like other types of reservations, these are growing smaller and fewer in face of the demand for roads and office space and parking lots.

In areas where families are small and neighbours tend to keep to themselves, it is entirely possible for a female to pass from kindergarten to menopause without ever being in charge of a baby—anybody's baby—for a single hour, and without ever having seen one suckled. Women's breasts as aesthetic objects feature pictorially in millions of newspapers every day, and there are places where people go to eat and drink enticed by the promise that the waitresses' breasts will be naked. But in any restaurant, if a customer dares publicly to use one of hers for the purpose for which it was designed, she encounters reactions of disgust and indignation. She may be quietly asked to choose between desisting and being evicted, because she is upsetting the clientele and putting them off their food.

The coming of affluence—because of its unequal distribution—has revealed another thing about women. Even if they want babies and feel warmly disposed to them, they do not want the job of looking after them for 24 hours a day if they can possibly avoid it. Those who can afford it hire nannies and nursemaids, and have always done so, long before there was any talk of using the time saved to develop their personalities or build a career for themselves. They did it because having sole charge of a young child for twenty-four hours a day is hard graft, especially where there are 'civilised' standards to be kept up. It was easier in some ways when there was only a grass hut.

So, although today's women are not isolate-reared like the hapless rhesus monkeys, their urban world lacks many of the social triggers which in the primates convert the potential for mother-love into an active reality.

Young women whose motherhood becomes imminent are liable to feel that they are facing the unknown, and they are not entirely sure that they can cope with a baby. They go to classes to learn how to breathe. They ring up, out of the blue, old school friends who have been through this rite before them. They may even go to the length of questioning their own mothers, until they read the books and discover that their mothers did all the wrong things. Mother is surprised at this: she knows that it was grandmother who did all the wrong things.

The advice they were given in the nineteenth century was that the child was born full of sin and that the parents' sacred duty was to break its will and beat the devil out of it. (This was one aspect of child care in which many pious fathers showed a willingness to co-operate.) After the First World War there was less emphasis on sin and more on pragmatism. Social changes had led to a chronic servant shortage, the supply of nannies and governesses shrank alarmingly, and many thousands of young, literate, middle-class women were faced with the prospect of hands-on baby care, and no idea how to go about it.

The manuals addressed to them by professional child carers laid a lot of stress on gaining the upper hand in the battle of wills between mother and child. Picking up a baby simply because it wanted to be picked up, or feeding it fifteen minutes ahead of the proper feeding time, was letting the side down and laying up trouble for the future. The correct procedure was to show it who was going to be boss by letting it cry its heart out until the clock struck.

It was a great relief when, after the Second World War, Dr Spock released mothers from this strait-jacket. He told them to relax and trust their instincts. If the baby wanted a cuddle and mum wanted to oblige, she had Dr Spock's permission to go ahead and cuddle. They loved him for it. Unfortunately, after Spock's liberal attitudes induced him to oppose the Vietnam war, there was a great campaign to denigrate him and all his works. He was accused of being personally responsible for the permissive society, the decline in public morals and the break-up of the family. Under pressure, he allowed that maybe he had gone too far. But, then, under pressure, Galileo allowed that the sun goes round the world.

In the 1970s there was another shift of emphasis. Animal researches, like Konrad Lorenz's studies of imprinting in geese and Harlow's experiments with isolate-reared monkeys, had led to new thinking on child rearing. The best and most authoritative account of what had been learned was embodied in John Bowlby's widely influential volumes on 'Attachment and Loss'. As summarised by himself, they pointed out that 'the young child's hunger for his mother's love and presence is as great as his hunger for food', that her absence inevitably generates 'a powerful sense of loss and anger', and that these traumas can inflict lasting damage. By chance, these publications coincided with the initial stages of a movement for women's liberation. Some of the people who were alarmed by Women's Lib used them to draw two disquieting conclusions.

One was a reinforced belief that anything that goes wrong with anybody anywhere can be blamed on the way their mothers brought them up. In a society beset with obscure feelings of guilt, and the desire to find someone on whom to off-load them now that Satan has retired, that message always finds a welcome. The second is that once a woman has borne a child, she has got to stick very close to it for at least the next three years for fear of inflicting irreparable psychological damage on it.

The pre-war message had been that you must never cuddle them too much or you will spoil them. Spock's message was that you and the child should play it by ear and work out a *modus vivendi* between you. The new message seemed to be that short of toting it everywhere in a papoose-carrier you can never give it enough contact-comfort, and that no one can ever deputise for you. It is worth checking what Bowlby actually said.

He was talking about imprinting or something very like it. When Lorenz published his findings on imprinting in newly hatched goslings, students of child behaviour could see no sign of anything resembling it in human babies, but that was because they were looking for it in the wrong place—in the new-born. Like several other phenomena—such as shivering and weeping and the descent of the larynx—its appearance is delayed, possibly because the baby is born at an immature stage of development.

It then emerged that 'attachment behaviour', which in some ways resembles imprinting, can be observed at around six months old. At that stage a baby can distinguish very clearly between its mother and any other human being, and forms an attachment to her. If separated from her, it shows signs of distress; if separated for a longer time it will display graver symptoms—anger, resentment, and something akin to shock or bereavement.

The observations are well documented. The cases, naturally at that date, almost all consisted of babies who had been brought up by their mothers in their own homes. In some cases when the mother brought her baby to the clinic the father came too. Presumably the kind of partner who does this is the kind who takes an active interest in his child. It was observed that when this is the case and the father goes out of the room, the baby manifests precisely the same kind of anxiety as when the mother goes out of the room, and the same kind of pleasure when he returns. It was also shown that if the mother is absent—even for a considerable time, perhaps in hospital—the child is less upset if he is with someone he knows, even if it is a sibling too young to look after him.

Bowlby himself could not have put it more clearly: 'Almost from the first many children have more than one figure towards whom they direct attachment behaviour' and 'The role of the child's principal attachment figure can be filled by others than the natural mother'.

The other conclusion he reached was that the person most likely to be selected by the infant to fulfil that role was not necessarily the one who fed him or gave him presents. What 'determined most clearly the figures to whom the child would become attached were the speed with which a person responded to an infant and the intensity of interaction in which he engaged with that infant'. In Arthur Miller's resonant phrase: 'Attention, attention must finally be paid.'

The mother does not have to carry the full load. Others can share it with her if they are available, if they are around soon enough, often enough, involved enough. But a child constantly straight-armed by preoccupied parents, plus a quick succession of auxiliary strangers, is liable to turn into a sullen adolescent with a residue of resentment that takes many years to die away.

19

Before Language

'A child is not just a half-formed adult.' Few people would disagree in principle with that statement by child psychologist N. Blurton Jones, but in practice it is not easy to cure ourselves of thinking of children in those terms.

For example, we note that a human child between three and four months of age becomes more vocal and spends more of his waking time babbling, at a time when a chimpanzee infant is becoming more silent; and we tend to conclude that he babbles because in future he must learn to speak. We note that he shows more curiosity in the manipulation of objects than apes of the same age; and we tend to conclude that this is because in the future he must learn how to wield tools and utensils.

However, it is equally possible to look at these facts from a different angle, and consider that verbal communication is likelier to arise in a species whose infants have occasion to babble; and the abilities to make and deploy tools will develop faster in a species whose infants have the habit of manipulating objects.

There are some reasons for suggesting that the latter may be a more fruitful approach. One is that it may throw some light on why humans developed along such different lines from the chimpanzee and the gorilla. To the layman it seems obvious that we became smarter because it would improve our chances of survival. To a scientist that proposition is less self-evident. The fact is that very little is known about the selective value of human intelligence.

An adult hominid venturing out of the forest would not be confronted by problems essentially different from those encountered by an adult chimpanzee. But, if scientists are right in thinking that the infants of *Homo erectus* were being born in a relatively immature state, then those infants would be confronted with radically different problems from those of the other primate infants, and their brains would be likely to develop along different lines in several pertinent respects.

An infant primate of any species is laying down pathways and connections in his brain which constitute the basic ground plan for the lines along which it will later become specialised. What he is doing, in a more active and literal sense than he can do in later years, is making— or making up—his mind. He makes repeated use of those faculties available to him, to exert an influence on his environment and attain his desires. A human baby, having far more limited physical powers in his first year, is forced to make greater use of other faculties, in the same way as hearing becomes more acute and discriminating in people who are born blind.

If we regard the matter from this perspective, it is perfectly possible to explain most of the things a baby does without ever resorting to the assumption that it is rehearsing for its future role as an adult.

For example, an infant gorilla or chimpanzee wanting to suckle can, when it is two weeks old, climb up to the teat and cling to its mother's fur unaided. Its clinging instinct is so powerful that if a young ape infant is put down to sleep alone in a basket, its hands may grip one another, or grip its feet, so tightly that it seems unable to undo them unless the human carer helps to prise the digits apart.

But for months, a human baby wanting to suckle can neither climb onto his mother nor cling to her. The only way he can affect the issue is by maximising eye-contact and interaction with his mother. For this interaction it is an advantage for human faces to become more expressive, and as Darwin pointed out in *The Expression of the Emotions in Man and Animals*, this is one of the diagnostic differences between humans and other primates.

Similarly, if an ape or a monkey moves away, her infant can scramble after her and climb onto her again. A human baby cannot even lift his head to try to see where she is. But he soon learns that she can hear him uttering sounds and will often reply to him, so that he knows she is near. An ape infant separated from its mother will automatically scream a protest—an involuntary and stereotyped reaction like all vocalisations in apes. The babbling of an infant, however, is not an unconditioned reflex. He practises it on his own and when he is not in distress. He is learning to make conscious use of vocal powers for his immediate advantage, not for the sake of the adult he will one day become. The sounds of his mother's voice are a behavioural reward and a reassurance, long before he can understand what she is saying.

Primates, like most mammals, are born with a powerful instinct to investigate objects with their noses and mouths, primarily to ascertain whether they are good to eat. From birth, or soon after, they are capable of going up to an object that interests them, sniffing it, picking it up in their mouths.

A human baby cannot go up to anything. The most distant object he can reach is the length of his arm away, and the only tool he has for lessening the distance between himself and the object is his hand. He still has the instinct to investigate objects with his mouth, but even for this manoeuvre his hand has to act as intermediary.

Once he can sit up and reach for an object, his reactions are different from an ape's of the same age. The young ape will often mouth it without using his hands at all. He may give it a push, to determine whether it is alive or not, and whether it is a separate object or stuck to the ground;

he may lift it in one hand and put it down again before going on to something else.

The human infant's attention span is longer, conceivably because at this age he has not yet got the option of moving on to something else, so it pays him to extract the maximum information and entertainment value from the thing he has already got. He will lift it, turn it over, view it from different angles, pass it from one hand to another and back again. If he has been accustomed to a rattle he will shake it to see if it makes a noise. If he has been accustomed to boxes he will try to find out whether it will open or change its shape or come apart.

Other pathways in his brain, that in other primates are concerned with improving and perfecting locomotion, cannot be activated yet because he is for so long incapable of locomotion. Priority is therefore given to improving control over the functioning of his hands, his features, and his vocal cords. The fact that he may become a tool maker or an orator is not the cause of the way he utilises his mind; it is more likely to be the effect.

A survey of primate social development edited by Suzanne Chevalier-Skolnikoff and Frank Poirier compared the early development of human children with that of various other primates. One of the most consistently striking findings was the initial and sustained responsiveness of human neonates to the human voice and, to a lesser extent, the human face.

This was not because the face belonged to the same species in the case of the human, and an alien one in the case of the chimpanzee. In a study by Martha B. Hallock, of chimpanzee new-borns, it was recorded that for at least the first seven days after birth, they were never seen to look at their mother's face at all. This may be partly because their mothers do not look at the infants' faces. When the first set of tests was repeated three weeks later at twenty-three days, the chimps which had been reared by humans showed a marked increase in social responsiveness, and those which had been left with their mothers showed no increase at all.

The range of expressions by means of which the human face conveys emotions and intentions is so important, especially in pre-verbal interactions, that special facial muscles have evolved, unique to our species. Other primates can raise and lower their eyebrows, but they cannot move them together in a frown, or elevate their inner ends in the circumflex position expressive of puzzlement or dismay, or form the 'pucker face' which, in a human infant, is the signal that he may be going to cry. Some of them can raise the outer ends of their lips in a grin or 'play face', but they cannot turn them down to express gloom. If a species of monkey has a mouth turned down at the edges, that expression is a fixture, like the smile on the face of a shark.

The baby soon shows it is capable of producing—and understanding, and reacting to—the standard range of human expressions. The smile is there from day one. It is certainly instinctive since it is seen in infants that are born blind. Equally certainly, it is not just a rictus of gastric discomfort as used to be claimed. Although it is innate, it very soon becomes used as a means of influencing people. This seems to be confirmed by one simple fact.

Most people have observed that if an infant is crying and somebody picks him up, more often than not he stops. Fewer people have observed that if he is smiling winningly to charm someone into picking him up, again more often than not, when they do pick him up, he stops smiling. Presumably for the same reason: the smile, like the crying, had been a method of communication and a means to an end.

Unlike the physical movements known as body language, most of our facial expressions are found in all races of mankind, and most of them are spontaneously used by children, although some may be consciously discarded in later life. Pouting, for example, and biting the lower lip, come to be regarded as babyish and regressive, especially in males. One of the few new expressions acquired in the course of growing up is the sneer of contempt. It is said to be familiarity that breeds contempt; a young child, to whom everything in the world is new, would have no use for such an emotion.

Compared with facial expressions, gestures are more often culturally transmitted. Some, it is true, are part of the common ape inheritance, such as pushing, hugging, beckoning, kissing, holding hands or thrusting out the face as a sign of aggression. Scratching is a very ancient pattern behaviour found in most mammals, but only the apes also share our habit of scratching the head as a displacement activity when momentarily checked or baffled.

Apes are also given to thumb-sucking when in need of comfort. This gesture is seen in 80 per cent of ape infants not reared by their mothers. For several generations the conventional wisdom in human nurseries was that sucking on thumbs or comforters was an infantile vice, unhygienic because both thumbs and dummies might have been in contact with dirt, and harmful because it was believed to distort the development of the mouth and the teeth. Under the strictest régimes it was persecuted like masturbation, and mittens were tied on the hands to make it physically impossible. On this, as on many precepts, views have changed. Bowlby described the habit as an activity in its own right, and declared that 'the baby able to engage in non-nutritional sucking is likely to become more content and relaxed than one not able to'.

Among the gestures that we do not share with the apes, many—like nodding the head for 'Yes'—are widespread but not universal, so that travellers using sign language have to be wary. As Desmond Morris pointed out, gestures of the fingers and thumbs can convey embarrassingly different meanings in different parts of the world. And children's gestures that appear spontaneous are sometimes imitative: when a little girl stands with arms akimbo to administer a scolding, the chances are that she has seen her mother do it.

However, when a human gesture is both universal and unique to our species, it has usually been acquired in infancy. It is a hangover that we retain because it has become an easily recognised signal. Shaking the head always means no. It is not an anthropoid inheritance: a silver-backed gorilla shakes his head at subordinates as a gesture of reassurance: 'I am not going to harm you'.

In our own case, for anyone who has tried to give a baby a spoonful of something it does not want to eat, the origins of the gesture hold no mystery. It surely predates the invention of the spoon, but for millions of years at weaning time our omnivorous species has been trying to commend unfamiliar foods to its young by putting things into their mouths while their heads turn from side to side as an evasive action.

Pointing, too, is universal. It probably derives, firstly, from a baby's ineffectual attempt to reach an object, and then from observing that the gesture often results in drawing someone else's attention to the object and perhaps handing it over.

There is one gesture made by the pre-school child which is rarely used in later life except by people interacting with children and unconsciously trying to empathise with them by re-enacting a long lost movement. It happens when one child goes up to another to console him if he is crying, to make an overture of friendship, or to borrow a toy and make sure the borrowing will not be resented. Before gazing into the other child's face, the head goes down to the side, almost on to the shoulder. It is distinctively human. It is at the opposite pole from all the agonistic animal poses intended to make the gesturer appear larger and more fearsome: the intention seems to be to appease by seeming smaller and harmless. Perhaps it is derived from trying to look into the face of someone who is smaller or whose head is bowed with unhappiness; but in practice it is not only directed at younger children or sad ones. If we could accept that the children are re-enacting behaviours once common to the whole human race, that would give us reason to believe that there really was a golden age of peace and harmony somewhere in our evolutionary past. The truth is that it is age specific, and probably means nothing except that the very young are weak and unsure of themselves, or perhaps they are nicer in some ways than we are. There is one other indication of it. They can get angry and push and slap and yell at one another, but although they can wield sticks and spades for purposes of play, the use of weapons, as students of child behaviour assure us, 'is not in their repertoire.'

One piece of universal human body language they have not acquired is the shrug. Perhaps it derives from the gesture of discarding a metaphorical load, and young children do not carry loads. It is used to convey such meanings as: 'I don't know, I don't care, there is nothing I can do about this,' or, in other words: 'You are overestimating my knowledge, my involvement, my power to influence events.' The pre-school child seldom has to deal with people who overestimate his power to influence events; in dealing with infants we are much more prone to underestimate them.

20

Talking

Apes, unlike humans, have never learned to speak and one scientist, when challenged to give a reason for this, returned a very brief answer: 'Because they have nothing to say.' It was not as flippant as it sounds. Primates are excellent communicators, able to transmit to one another all the information they feel the need to convey.

The oldest mammalian channel of communication is via olfactory signals, of a range and variety we are quite incapable of evaluating because our own capacity to smell is hopelessly attenuated. And while we have invented artificial means of augmenting our powers of sight and hearing, no one has yet marketed a smelling aid.

In the higher primates, olfactory messages are still powerful and essential in regulating sexual relationships but, in general, Old World apes and monkeys tend to rely less on scent and more on sight and sound. By means of movements of their mouths and eyebrows, subtle deployment of body language and personal space, and a variety of vocal signals, they can vividly express their emotions, warn others of danger, convey their own perception of their place in the social hierarchy, and signal their immediate intentions and desires. Jane Goodall counted 23 different sounds uttered by the Gombe chimpanzees.

In several primates, of which the vervet monkey is the best known example, the signals warning of danger have gained a further precision by specifying the particular

types of danger. Different sounds are uttered in response
to sighting a leopard, an eagle or a snake, causing the
other monkeys in the band to take the appropriate avoid-
ing action even if they have not seen the threat for themselves.

It is not easy to see how the ability of these primates to
survive would be enhanced by extending their already
adequate repertoire. Perhaps the vervets could invent a
special signal for: 'Look out!—Land-Rover', but nothing
would be gained by that. In the case of any large potential
threat rapidly approaching overland, the leopard call
would serve just as well, and result in the correct strategy
being adopted.

The most brilliant ape communicator to date, the pygmy
chimpanzee Kanzi, has shown an ability to understand
and respond to a wide range of words and sentences in
spoken English. He can carry out suggestions made to
him verbally. Given a keyboard covered with symbols, he
can inform an experimenter that he wants, or intends, to
go to a particular place and eat or play with a particular
item quite outside his present range of vision.

These achievements are a cause for wonder. They tell
us things we did not know about the mental capacity of
non-human primates, and they enable him to interact
more efficiently with human beings who can give him a
Coke when he asks for a Coke. But, as with the vervet
and the Land-Rover, there is no reason to believe that any
of his acquired abilities would help him to survive in his
native habitat, or to interact with his peers any more subtly
and efficiently than untaught apes already do.

Very young children—before they begin to speak or
even to babble—have, like young monkeys or apes, their
own repertoire of sounds. Scientists may not have
recorded and analysed the relative frequencies of babies'
cries as they have done with many animal and bird calls,
but a mother listening from the next room can interpret
their messages perfectly well.

She can tell if a baby is simply bored and tired and grizzling himself to sleep, or if he is hungry and getting hungrier by the minute and will not shut up until he is fed, or if something has happened demanding instant action. He cannot say that the cat has knocked an alarm clock off the shelf into the cot and hit him on the head, but he will certainly vary the pitch and frequency and volume of his cries effectively enough to bring her running.

The pitch of his utterance is in all cases higher than ours, but that is true of the young of most mammals. It is necessary for them to be different because their sounds require a different response. If an angry infant animal produced the same noise as an angry adult mammal, it might trigger the same knee-jerk response from a dominant male, and that could lead to bloodshed. Similarly, a squeak of alarm from a young monkey will not cause the whole band to disperse in panic as it might if it was pitched in a lower register.

The early baby noises, then, have everything in common with animal cries. They are involuntary: triggered off by an internal state or an outside event and not by a deliberate decision to communicate, any more than a gasp of surprise is, or a yelp of pain. They are innate, not imitated. We know this because if a baby or young animal is deaf, that does not prevent it from uttering the sounds characteristic of its species. And in new babies the sounds are identical in whatever part of the world they are born.

But at some time between three and four months of age, without relinquishing the use of these spontaneous utterances, the human baby begins to emit new sounds. They interest him in the same way as the new-born is interested in the movement of his own hand. He has already discovered that banging with a spoon or shaking a rattle will invariably produce a distinctive sound. He now discovers that he has a reliable method of producing a noise without using a hand at all: it is something you do in your throat. He lies there and practises it. When a syllable emerges, he tends to repeat it as he repeats the banging of the spoon, confirming that the relationship between what he has done and what he hears is not an arbitrary one. He gets the feedback: this noise is indeed coming out of him. His mother or carer seems pleased with his new achievement and talks or babbles back to him, which provides further reinforcement.

Stage two, after the babbling, is imitation. He hears a syllable: he recognises it as one of the sounds he can produce himself.

It seems a simple thing, not calling for a high level of intelligence, but this is the stage that the most brilliant among the anthropoid communicators will never spontaneously achieve. As long as research into their capacity for language consisted of trying to make apes speak, it demanded years of patient effort. The American psychologists K. J. and Caroline Hayes tried hard for six years to teach their chimp Vicky to speak, and the results were meagre in the extreme: an uncertain delivery by the animal of the words 'pa', 'up' and 'cup'.

It is not because a chimpanzee cannot attach meanings to words; it is not because it lacks the will to please. It is not because an ape that can smack its lips—as it frequently does—lacks the oral equipment for forming the consonant 'p'.

But, oftener than not, when it smacks its lips, any air passing through them is going in instead of out. It cannot co-ordinate what its lungs are doing with what its lips are doing, because it has no voluntary control over its breathing.

It is not easy to determine precisely to what extent any animal behaviour is voluntary. In 1968 Vernon Reynolds felt safe in declaring: 'All the calls of apes are involuntary expressions.' Some later writers express it more cautiously: 'Apes have limited voluntary control of vocalisation.' This does not mean that an ape can diversify its performances by uttering new sounds that are outside the fixed repertoire of its species. But, for example, having uttered a cry of rage and noted that it had a satisfying influence on the behaviour of others, it can reproduce it voluntarily by, as it were, lowering the threshold of anger which was originally needed to give rise to it.

What is certain is that the gap between apes and humans in this respect is immense and apparently unbridgeable. For human infants, vocal utterances are within their powers to produce, repeat, vary and modulate at will from an early age. Other primates never attain this power.

When a baby begins to babble, it picks up the tune of the language it hears around it in everyday life, before it learns any of the words. While the cry of the new-born is the same everywhere, the babbling of a Chinese baby can be distinguished from that of an English baby. Primates, whose utterances are involuntary, are also influenced to some extent by the 'language' they hear around them in their infancy. For instance, rhesus monkeys and Japanese macaques, while fairly closely related, are separate species with separate vocal repertoires; but if their babies are interchanged at birth, the sounds they make will not be identical either to the vocabulary of their mothers or their foster mothers. This indicates that, like most animal behaviour, it is influenced partly by heredity and partly by environment. There is some indication that correlating the sounds made by the new-born may provide clues to the evolutionary relationships between related species.

In the case of humans, the ability to produce specific sounds at will is still a far cry from language, and one of the greatest mysteries in human evolution is how our species came to jump that gap. We know that by now the ability to learn a language is innate. Noam Chomsky expressed this in the strongest terms by saying that we evolved a 'language organ'.

This is not a physical organ that can be located and dissected, although there are particular areas of the brain which have special relevance to the understanding and/or the utterance of speech. But some natural propensity to understand the structure of language seems to be born in us. Children do not have to be 'taught' a language: they only have to hear it spoken around them. They acquire a grasp of the rules that govern it one at a time, and the sequence in which the rules become clear to them is the same in all languages. They make the same kind of grammatical errors in all languages at the same stage of the learning process—for example, making 'mistakes' which are more logical than adult current usage, such as forming plurals like 'mouses', and past tenses like 'runned'.

It is conceivable that language—like, perhaps, the use of fire or the riding of horses—was a cultural invention that emerged at one time, in one place, and all the languages in the world may have evolved from a single original tongue in the same way that French and Spanish and Portuguese and Italian evolved from Latin. In earlier centuries there used to be a concept that if a baby was brought up in isolation and incommunicado, he would spontaneously speak that original language. The truth is that he would not speak at all. Children born deaf do not speak because they cannot hear themselves or other people. In the few authenticated cases of children reared by animals, or in severe isolation, they may be taught later in life to recognise words and imitate some of them, but not to produce grammatically structured sentences.

However, there is another question that remains unanswered. If a group of children with normal hearing was raised without ever hearing adults speak—children of *Homo sapiens sapiens* in whom the 'language organ' is part of the genetic endowment—we do not know whether or not they would develop a language of their own. Every parent knows that babies invent their own words for things. A co-operative mother often feels that, in the early stages, encouraging communication is more important than a correct vocabulary. She will settle temporarily for the infant's coinages and talk 'baby talk'. If she has little company apart from the baby, she may find herself saying to a chance visitor: 'Pass me the yaya, will you?' referring perhaps to a toy lorry or a security blanket—some possession so treasured by the child that he could not wait for its 'right' name to be disclosed to him.

The instances of private language used by twins do not entirely settle this question. The Gibbons twins June and Jennifer in England, and a pair of twins called Poto and Cabengo, filmed in San Diego in 1977, provide examples of 'secret' languages which other people could not understand. In both cases the twins communicated with one another in very rapid, staccato bursts of speech. Slowed down tape-recordings revealed that the Gibbons girls were talking in English, and that Poto and Cabengo, with a bilingual background, spoke a distorted patois compounded of a mixture of English and German.

Some language theorists are convinced that the acquirement of language by children can have nothing at all to do with its acquirement by the human race. T. W. Deacon, for example, in the *Cambridge Encyclopedia of Human Evolution*, asserts that 'Early hominids would have used adult brains to produce an adult language.'

But would they? Everything we know about the apes leads us to believe that the older they get the more stereotyped their behaviour becomes and the less likely they are to introduce cultural innovations of any kind. The chimpanzees who used to cavort at the London Zoo's 'Chimp Tea Parties' were always the young ones. The urge to play fades quite early in an anthropoid's life. And the great puzzle about the origin of language has always been that in the very beginning it must have been too crude to be of much practical use. The young of an anthropoid species which had acquired control of its vocalisations could have practised making new noises and finding uses for them, just as young gorillas practise gymnastics in the branches.

There was a popular theory that man became intelligent

when he became carnivorous, because carnivores spend less of their time eating, so they have leisure hours in which to play and experiment and indulge their curiosity—which is, as often as necessity, the mother of invention. It is said, too, that the secret of humanity's success is the prolonged retention of a childlike openness to new experiences and ideas. But even among carnivores, the age group which does most of the playing does not consist of adults, and it is not easy to see why being childlike should be productive of innovation in everyone except children.

There are three points worth making in this connection. One is that when instinctive sound repertoires in primates differ radically between the infants and the adult—as, for example, in mouse lemurs and bush babies—the infant repertoire is always the more varied and extensive.

The second is that girls learn to speak sooner and more fluently than boys. This seems to suggest that ancestrally vocal communication was more important within the mother/infant relationship than it was in the case of other social relationships.

The third is that in the first four or five years of life a language—or even two or three languages simultaneously—can be acquired avidly and apparently without effort. From then on, new languages become harder to learn; and if no language is learned before the age of five, the ability to acquire one at all is severely impaired. This is not true of any other human skill.

In other words, adults are incapable of learning to speak. Only children can do it. It may conceivably be true that adults nevertheless invented speech but, if so, then some evidence must be advanced in support of the proposition. It is by no means self-evident. What adults are extremely good at is exploiting this tool acquired in childhood to pass on the accumulated knowledge of their later years to the children who come after them.

By this time, a great deal of research has been carried

out comparing the verbal capacity of apes and children by studying their responses to a series of instructions spoken by someone invisible to them. Valid comparisons can thus be made of what they are being asked to do, and the performance of a clever anthropoid like the bonobo Kanzi is not far behind that of a two-year-old child. But there comes a time when such experiments run into a snag. Consider the following scenario.

A scientist sets up an experiment comparing the cognitive powers of Subject A, a chimpanzee, and Subject B, a child of the same age, presenting each of them in turn with identical tasks to perform. He says: 'Now put the *ball* into the *yellow* box'.

He records in his notebook: 'Subject A complies. Subject B says, "Why?"'

It is a cosmic moment. Subject A—even if it is Kanzi—is never going to ask that question. Give him a symbol for it on his lexigram cards and it will be meaningless to him. But from a child you will hear, according to Rudyard Kipling's poetic estimate, 'seven million whys'—and few parents will reckon that he exaggerated. The infant asks this question before he knows quite what it means. The other interrogatives are easier to understand, but they get terse answers, 'Where?'—'Over there.' 'What's that?'— 'A tin opener.' But 'Why' often elicits a long string of words, starting with 'Because . . .'. People treat this word more earnestly; they are more likely to make eye contact, to see whether their answer is understood. So this word is great fun to use. At first, at the end of the answer, young children say 'Why?' again, as if they thought the word meant, 'Go on, talk to me some more about that.' This ploy is subject to the law of diminishing returns. In any conversation, if a sequence of three 'becauses' is followed by a further 'Why?', the discussion begins to enter realms of philosophical profundity that would tax the powers of a Wittgenstein. The adult shows signs of irritation and will play the game no longer.

But in the end, after hundreds of thousands of examples, the penny drops. It does not mean 'tell me more'. It means that the universe as perceived by the adults of his own species is not chaotic: there are causes and effects. Adults believe that their own behaviour is not a series of ungovernable appetites and reflexes, but is mediated by their own understanding of the consequences of their actions. They make it clear that the child will be expected to behave in the same way.

Once the child has learned the meaning of 'why' and 'because', he has become a fully paid-up member of the human race.

21

Walking

During the second six months of his life the child concentrates much of his attention on his hands and his voice; his physical prowess lags far behind that of the chimpanzee.

He had to wait twenty-eight weeks before he could raise his head, which the chimp can do at four weeks. He had to wait twice as long as the chimp before he could sit up steadily, or roll over from lying on his back to lying on his tummy.

But at somewhere around eight months he may pull himself upright by holding the bars of his cot. A few weeks later he may begin to crawl. Timing varies widely between different children, but by his first birthday he will have passed, or is fast approaching, two of the milestones of human development—his first intelligible words and his first unaided steps.

A human child crawls on his hands and knees. This is a very unusual mode of locomotion which young gorillas and chimpanzees do not indulge in: they crawl on their hands and feet. The child's front limbs are relatively shorter. The length of his whole arm from shoulder to wrist is roughly similar to the length of the top part of his leg, from hip to knee. So, in order to keep his spine horizontal as any normal quadruped does, he lets the femur take the strain; the bottom half of his legs contributes nothing to his progress, but simply gets dragged along behind him.

For adult humans crawling on hands and knees quickly becomes uncomfortable and laborious. In an experiment with 31 volunteers who were asked to walk on hands and knees on a treadmill, their rate of respiration increased to over three times above the resting rate, more than twice as much as it would have if they had been walking on two legs. Their heart rate and temperature rose about three times as much as in bipedal walking.

In 'intermediary' infants—that is, at the stage in which they can walk on either two limbs or four—the increased energy demands of quadrupedalism are slight, in the region of 20 per cent as compared with the adults' 200 per cent. Morever, infants can crawl in this way quite easily with their heads held up to see where they are going. The adults found difficulty in sustaining this posture, and after five minutes they all complained of headache and sweating over the head and back of the neck.

In quadrupedal mammals the ratios work in the opposite direction: a dog can be trained to walk on two legs, but as measured by its respiration it finds bipedalism three times as laborious as its normal gait. Thus a man and his dog are both locomotor specialists, while the baby inhabits a grey area keeping both options open.

Habitual bipedalism as practised by humans is unique among mammals and has therefore proved very difficult to explain. For this reason the problem is often played down—as with human hairlessness and human subcutaneous fat—by saying that this is not a real distinction, but merely a matter of degree: other primates are part-time bipedalists whereas, in our case, bipedalism is habitual.

It is perfectly true that many primates can walk a short distance on two legs. Gorillas make bipedal charges as part of their dominance display; Japanese macaques can easily be trained to walk on two legs as a circus trick. A gibbon's main mode of locomotion is by swinging beneath the branches, but if ever it has occasion to proceed along the tops of them or on the rare occasions when it comes to earth, it usually opts to run along on two legs with its very long arms held out horizontally to help keep its balance. Physiologically, primate bipedalism is so different from ours that some scientists feel that the two modes should be given different names to distinguish them, but the potential for locomotion on two legs is undoubtedly there.

The young chimpanzee Gua was hand raised and given the same treatment as a human child, even to the extent of being given shoes to wear. In these circumstances she learned to walk bipedally, holding the hand of her carer, at about the same age as a child does. As with other innovative behaviours, upright walking even in the wild is commonest among the youngsters. For a short while, like human infants, they may be ambivalent about it. Sometimes, even in the wild, a gorilla mother has been seen playing with her infant, holding both its hands and retreating backwards as a human mother does when encouraging her child to walk.

But the practice leads nowhere: it is only a stopgap. African apes have their own unique locomotor speciality: knuckle walking. Once their infants have got the hang of that, they soon find they are able to gallop along and cover the ground very fast. The experiments with bipedalism are discontinued, and by the time they are fully grown, gorillas spend no more than two per cent of their time moving on two legs.

That is simple enough to understand. The young chimp selects the option which comes most easily to it. The child is in a different situation, showing remarkable persistence in acquiring a gait which does not come easily to him at all. When he can walk only with assistance, he will cry to have his hands held so that he can practise. And when the time comes for him to go it alone, he goes it alone in the face of a rather surprising deterrent: whereas a young chimpanzee walking bipedally never falls down, a one-year-old human walking bipedally falls down nearly as often as he says 'Why?'

Apes and monkeys moving bipedally all walk with their feet apart, their knees bent at all times, their bottoms sticking out, and their torsos inclined at an angle so that they are leading with their heads. Their mode of walking is not particularly elegant and it uses up more energy than human adult walking, but it does mean that the centre of gravity is nearer the ground and their weight is distributed more widely around it; both of these factors give more stability. Also, an ape's arms are so long that its hands hang down below its knees and are quite close to the ground. So any momentary imbalance would not result in a fall, merely in a steadying hand or knuckle being brought into play, or else a brief relapse into quadrupedalism.

The human baby's progress is far more precarious. The first steps of a one-year-old are made with stiff legs, and arms held out to the side. He has not learned how to put his feet down heel first—they are slapped down flat at every step, the toes clenched as if trying to get a purchase on whatever substrate he may be walking on. The footprints he leaves are very far from parallel—they point away from one another at an angle of anything up to 90 degrees. In the first weeks of unsupported walking he makes on average two or three steps before he loses his balance.

When this happens he has not yet acquired the instinct to throw his hands forward to protect his face as adults do when they trip and fall. The baby simply falls—sometimes backward onto his bottom, sometimes forward, banging his head. The damage is not serious, because he is so short that he doesn't have far to fall, but he is affronted, and yells, and is probably picked up and comforted.

This happens over and over again. In most laboratory experiments with animals, if any action is persistently followed by a short sharp shock, it sets up a conditioned reflex inhibiting the repetition of that action. It would not be surprising if, after the fifteenth bang on his head, the baby decided the game was not worth the candle. Instead, he wriggles out of the arms of his comforter and slides to the ground, hell-bent on trying again. Robert the Bruce did not need to study a spider to learn a lesson in pertinacity. Any one-year-old baby would have provided him with an equally good model.

This intermediary baby is not intrinsically forced to plug away at bipedalism: he could simply carry on crawling. Indeed, if his objective is to reach something rather than showing off his new trick, he will promptly drop to the ground and scuttle across the room on all fours, because it is faster and easier.

Remembering the young ape Gua happily trudging along in her nice new shoes, it seems clear that the child's indefatigable attempts to walk upright are largely a matter of education. He has a powerful urge to imitate our actions as well as our intonations, and while every failure in walking is punished with a slap from Mother Earth, success gives him the approval of his own kind.

How would he make his way around if he did not have our example constantly before his eyes? Accounts of feral children are not the most reliable source of data, but there is an account of the 'wolf children of Midnapore' in a diary kept by the Rev J.A.L. Singh in 1920, corroborated by documents from the orphanage to which the girls were taken and by a few box camera photographs. According to this diary 'Kamala and Amala could not walk like humans'. When first found they were covered with 'sores all over the body. These sores ate up the big and extensive corns on the knee and on the palms of the hands near the wrist which had developed from walking on all fours'.

When the advantages of bipedalism are weighed against the disadvantages, one of the items on the debit side has to be waiting longer for the young to become efficiently mobile. The one thing we know is that long ago there must have been a time for our distant ancestors, as there is now briefly for our children, when they came to a development crossroads. On the vital question of four legs versus two legs, the apes went one way and the hominids went the other. Robert Frost could have been speaking for all humanity when he wrote:

> Two roads diverged in a wood, and I –
> I took the one less traveled by,
> And that has made all the difference.

22

The Peer Group

When James Thurber was instructed by his botany professor to draw the plant cells mounted on the slide of
a microscope, he repeatedly declared that he could see
nothing. Having tried with every adjustment of the microscope known to man, he drew what he finally saw, and
his exasperated professor looked at the drawing.

'He bent over and squinted into the microscope. His
head snapped up. "That's your eye!" he shouted. "You've
fixed the lens so that it reflects. You've drawn your eye!"'

One thing that makes it so hard to study *Homo sapiens*
scientifically is that, at whatever angle we fix the lens, we
are looking at ourselves. Not only the answers we come
up with, but the very questions we ask about ourselves
are largely dictated by the kind of people we are and the
kind of society we live in.

In the aftermath of the Second World War there was a
preoccupation with the causes of aggression, and specu-
lations about prehistoric hominids depicted them princi-
pally as slayers of beasts and men. When the traditional
nuclear family seemed to be a permanent fact of life, they
were seen as monogamous breadwinners, carrying food
to their mates and offspring. At a time when sociology
was concerned with class differences, and business studies
with the personal problems of Organisation Man, animal
studies focused on pecking orders and dominance hierarchies and the role of the alpha male.

Just as the perspective of the researchers changes, so human behaviour also changes—with increasing speed as time goes by. Within the present century, the behaviour of people of different generations may vary as widely as that of people from different cultures. It becomes ever more difficult to make statements about human social relationships which are true for the whole human species and not for one geographical or chronological subsection.

Three methods are often applied by way of checking how far such statements can be accepted as universally valid. One is by collecting and comparing data about people from different parts of the world and different levels of civilisation. Another is by cross-species studies: if a particular behaviour pattern is displayed by other primates as well as ourselves, we can be confident that it has a strong genetic component. And the third is by studying groups of pre-school children interacting spontaneously together. At that stage they are mobile enough to do their own thing, but in terms of conforming to an imposed social etiquette they remain comparatively unbrainwashed.

In every primate species there comes a time when the infants show a disposition to spend more time away from the immediate vicinity of the mother and take an interest in other animals near to their own age. In the wild, this separation is instigated by the young at their own chosen time and pace; in the peer groups studied by child psychologists the timing is less flexible. It tends to be institutionalised as entry into a nursery school or playgroup for a fixed number of hours per day in—as it might be—the 'class of '94'.

Among chimpanzees, Jane Goodall observed that for the first year an infant is rarely out of contact with its mother, but by 18 months of age the habit of wandering off to play with young companions is well established. In children it is generally agreed that this landmark is not passed until they are about three years old.

From that point on, the peer group experience is invaluable. The behavioural studies of Harlow and Harlow in the 1950s showed that the social ineptitude displayed by isolate-reared rhesus monkeys could be dramatically reduced by permitting them to play with other young monkeys. Even being allowed to watch others playing without actually taking part made them less withdrawn, and free access to playmates went a very long way towards cancelling out the damage done by their initial experience of motherlessness.

In past centuries very few children were deprived of the opportunity of such play. In the days of large families, a good deal of the hands-on socialisation process was in practice carried out by other children of varying ages, with parent(s) functioning largely as courts of appeal. In deprived urban areas the streets—before they were commandeered by the motor car—were open playgrounds of which the children were the undisputed owners during the hours while fathers were in work and mothers at home.

Among such multi-age groups whole cultures can grow up transmitted by children to children, cultures with their own protocol, and rules, and games. Adults may pass on to their children the rules of cricket or baseball, but other children teach them the rules of skipping games and hopscotch. Adults sing nursery rhymes, in which Little Boy Blue and Little Bo Peep still follow their woolly flocks, to babies who will probably never encounter a live sheep. But there is a parallel set of rituals and oral traditions passed on from child to child—some of them captured and recorded (none too soon) by people like the Opies—in which the songs are sometimes more ribald, and always less ossified, more likely to incorporate newer facts of life like the cinema, the football pools, and television.

These phenomena, insofar as they have been studied at all, have been treated as the province of art rather than science. Multi-age groups of juvenile humans are too inchoate and uncontrollable to be the subject of detailed scientific study. Analysis is more easily applied in the case of groups which are smaller, more homogeneous and, to all intents and purposes, captive. A playgroup or nursery group of three-to-five-year-olds fits the bill very nicely.

There used to be a belief that just as the embryo recapitulates some of the features of far distant animal ancestors, so children's mental development and social development must recapitulate early stages of social organisation—that is, that children begin as savages, develop into barbarians, and only finally grow into civilised beings. Rousseau believed they were barbarians until the age of twelve, and that any attempts at formal education should be postponed until that date. Infants were studied in the hope that they would teach us things about our own prehistory—meaning, of course, the prehistory of adults.

They teach us nothing of the kind. In this connection, as in others, it was necessary for evolutionists like P.E. Davidson to point out the basic facts: that 'early stages of all organisations evolve to meet their own necessities', that 'infancy probably has had its own evolution', and that 'their ancestral reference would be first to ancestral infancies and only indirectly to adult characters'.

With this proviso, infants can teach us a few things about the human nature that we share with them. They teach us something, for example, about dominance relationships—not a lot, because awareness of their relative status among their peers does not emerge until the age of about six. But in long-term studies of a particular group it is possible for researchers to identify individual children with potential qualities of 'leadership'—traits which make it likely that when a pecking order does emerge, they will be at the top of it. It is interesting that the children who later turn out to be leaders are not those who initially show most aggression, but the ones who show the most appeasing, conciliatory, friendly behaviour in the early stages. Studies of baboons led to a similar conclusion: those who ended up as alphas were not the ones with a low flashpoint, but those who successfully avoided getting into any fights until they were big enough to be quite sure of winning.

Children can also teach us a little about the nature of human aggression, although they do not normally display aggression before the age of three. This is not seen, as it was once, as a relic of an idyllic bygone age in human prehistory, but as reflecting the fact that up to that point their mothers will display on their behalf any aggression that may be necessary.

Child studies made some contribution to dispelling a once popular theory that aggression was an inbuilt 'drive'—that a fixed amount of it was generated which, in the interests of health, had to find an outlet, rather like the output of the sweat glands. It was felt that failure to display or 'act out' overt aggression must necessarily mean that it was being unhealthily bottled up and turning inwards, sowing the seeds of future neuroses.

This theory remains unproven. Aggression is a response to specific stimuli—such as frustration or being aggressed against—in the same way as scratching or vomiting are responses to stimuli. There may be a genetic component in the readiness with which aggression is triggered off, but there can be no doubt that the amount of aggression displayed by an individual animal (or child) is closely connected with the amount of frustration or aggression to which it has been subjected. This conclusion was also confirmed by experiments with rats. Two strains of rats were selected, one strain far more aggressive than the other. But when infants from the two strains were cross-fostered, their behaviour as they grew up reflected the behaviour of the fostering community more closely than that of their genetic parents.

Since physical aggression between members of the same species is a costly and often dangerous pattern of behaviour, natural selection favours the evolution of social strategies like appeasement signals which diffuse anger and reduce the incidence of conflict. Young children have evolved their own social strategies which are not quite like ours, and not quite like those of any other primate infants. One unique aspect is the important role which is played by the giving and receiving of objects. Friendly overtures in a pre-school playgroup very often consist of approaching a playmate and holding out a toy.

The same approach may be used in relation to adults— a toddler may establish contact by bringing some small object and putting it into the lap or into the hand of a visitor as a way of attracting attention.

This is one manifestation of a strategy already emergent in chimpanzees. An individual chimpanzee may be uncertain of its ability to obtain high ranking by menacing or aggressive behaviour. In that case it can often improve its status by other attention-getting devices—doing tricks and 'showing off'. Children do the same thing, often accompanied by cries of 'Look at me.'

Michael Chance christened this kind of tactic 'hedonic' as opposed to the 'agonic mode' of threats, counter-threats and appeasement gestures. Offering-behaviour by children can be a specialised human variation of the hedonic approach.

This behaviour develops naturally from the important part played by manipulation in the first year of the child's development. As a social strategy it works very well. The child receiving the object will examine it with interest, and the mental procedures involved in the investigation tend to suppress the hormones associated with fear and aggression. Parents show their understanding of this when they try—often successfully—to quieten a screaming infant by drawing its attention to something new and interesting.

In the nursery class the giving is often a spontaneous gesture. Or it may be the response to a request, provided that the request is made in the appropriate manner which entails in this age group the smile, the head on one side, the hand held out to receive the object, the upward inflexion in the voice.

However, if an object is taken away by force without the preliminary ritual, the child reacts strongly with a crying face, a howl of dismay, and in extreme cases a deliberate collapse onto the floor. (The last gesture is a common one among all frustrated primate infants, designed to arouse maternal concern by pretending to be at death's door. Even among monkeys, the mother is rarely fooled.)

Many attempts have been made over the years to distil into one phrase the essence of what makes humans different—do they represent the hunting ape? the naked ape? the tool-making ape? In view of the very early ontogenic development of the sense of being in possession of material objects, and the overwhelming part it has played in our economic history, it is mildly surprising that no one has suggested the property-owning ape. In the infant's vocabulary, 'mine' is a word that is acquired early and employed loudly and often.

There is no clear parallel to this range of behaviour in any other species. In non-human animals the sense of ownership is only exhibited in respect of food and territory, and in respect of social relationships. Males in harem-type or monogamous societies behave as if the females belonged to them, and females and young generally behave possessively towards one another.

When 'giving' behaviour is observed, what is given is never an object but always food—usually to the young, sometimes to females. In some penguin species a male occasionally presents his mate with a pebble, but this seems not so much a gift from A to B as the kind of symbolic contribution to nest-building found in many species; it may be a hangover from a time when penguins lived in less extreme climates and still built some kind of nest.

The giving-and-taking strategy is clearly adaptive, not only because it promotes friendly relations, but because an object which has aroused the interest of one child will be passed around and handled by others; in prehistoric contexts when interesting objects were less thick on the ground than they are in a nursery class, it would serve to enrich the experience of all.

But when it misfires, it can lead to conflict. A child from whom an object is taken without permission becomes cross. A child who has solicited an object with all due ceremony, and has been refused, may also become cross.

There is no evidence from this age group for the theory that language developed as a means of furthering social harmony. The squabbling of young children is a silent affair. Any vocabulary they have acquired goes out of their minds when they become angry; their fights, unlike those of adults, are seldom preceded and never accompanied by verbal abuse. They may grab, pinch, slap, scratch or bite; a sudden push in the chest is a favourite manoeuvre because all of them are beginners at bipedality and easily destabilised.

By the age of five the incidence of physical assault is considerably reduced. This appears to be because a dominance structure has by this time become fairly well established. A symbolically raised arm or—in 30 per cent of cases—merely a threatening look from a recognised superior in the pecking order can decide the outcome of a conflict of interests without a word being spoken, and without anyone actually getting biffed.

As in other species, those who cannot gain their ends by physical superiority sometimes prevail by exercising other tactics—appeasement, patience, guile, the formation of alliances, or an appeal for protection from a higher authority, whether an alpha male or a nursery teacher.

By now it has become clear that we cannot follow our hypothetical infant into this milieu without abandoning the use of the arbitrary pronoun 'he'. We have entered the territory of what the legend over the school door used to call 'mixed infants'. These children come in two kinds, and by this time they are well aware of it. The question of when and how they become aware of it has been at the heart of a long-running debate about heredity versus environment as the main factor governing gender differences in status and behaviour.

For a period there was a tendency for the nature/nurture debate to become polarised by sexual politics. The feminists laid stress on social engineering as the main source of differences in behaviour; their opponents pointed out that dominance in males and submission by females was part of our primate inheritance. It was a fruitful debate, in that it stimulated research into such questions as the complex inter-relationships between hormone levels and behaviour and life experience.

In this connection study of the behaviour of young children and their parents was highly relevant. The 'nature' school pointed out that little boys preferred to play with guns, and little girls with dolls. The 'nurture' school argued that they were brought up to do so; these were the toys they were given. The 'nature' school countered with evidence that boys were more adventurous even before they were old enough to play with guns or to be coached in gender roles, or even to understand language.

The nurturists responded with a classic experiment in which a baby was left for a time in the care of adults and their reactions were studied. Their behaviour towards it differed significantly according to whether they had been told it was a boy or a girl. The determining factor must therefore be cultural, and a product of human social engineering.

There followed yet another turn of the screw. Primatologists reported that when an infant ape is born in the wild, the primate group displays quite as much eagerness as humans do to determine whether it is male or female. They peer and sniff at its genitals. And the mother regulates her own behaviour according to whether she is dealing with a male or female infant. She is more protective of the females, keeps them closer to her for a longer period; she is rougher with male babies, more likely to fend them off and rebuff their advances and encourage their independence. So if our differential methods of rearing are indeed cultural, they are part of ape as well as of human culture.

A final and so far definitive experiment has been repeated with the same result on three different occasions by different teams on different sets of babies. It is very simple: it consists of counting the smiles of babies within the first twenty-four hours after birth. The people who do the counting are not told the sex of the babies. A baby girl smiles more readily than a baby boy. No one is likely to argue about that. Latter-day feminists tend to take their stand on a different platform from that of their grandmothers, maintaining not that there is no difference between innate male and female behaviour patterns, but that female behaviour is more, rather than less, civilised: a more tenable hypothesis.

Male infants tend to be bigger and more aggressive, slower at learning to speak, and not so good at manipulation where it calls for precision rather than brute force. Little girls make rather more use of the infantile appeasement signals. This may be partly a consequence of the fact that they are smaller—appeasement in both sexes and all primates is preferentially directed towards those who are big enough to push them around—but the smiles of the new-born suggest that a genetic compound is also involved. In later life, when males have outgrown the head-on-one-side appeasement signal, girls and women may still make unconscious use of it when they are in a conciliatory mood.

In the first months at play school or nursery class, the boys cry just as much as the girls do, but the incidence of thumb-sucking is seven times higher among the girls. There is a possibility that in humans, as in apes, the biological clock dictates that the 'right' time for infants to spend time away from their mothers is later in females than in males. The occasional mother who insists: 'I'm not sending her yet—she's not ready' may be prompted by a sound instinct. On the other hand, it may be a mistake to assume that more thumb-sucking is a sign of more distress at being away from mother: prenatal thumb-sucking, whatever its cause, can hardly be a response to separation. It could be that the girls choose this response to being in an unfamiliar situation in preference to making a noisier kind of fuss.

Among the peer groups in the nursery class and in the primary school, boys and girls have one striking characteristic in common—a tendency to forgather with others of their own sex and regard the opposite sex with disfavour, derision, and often outspoken contempt. Girls do not voluntarily seek the company of nasty, rough boys; boys avoid hanging around with girls because they are well known to be soppy. From nursery class onwards, these attitudes strengthen. It is not inculcated behaviour; juvenile primates also tend to play in single-sex groups. In apes, as in humans, the young males' play is more rough and tumble, and more likely to be conducted in gangs. It is not easy to see how this voluntary sexual segregation could be regarded as a preparation for adult life.

The time will come when their biological clocks will strike. For most of the boys and most of the girls, the opposite sex will come to exert a curious fascination. The progenitive urge will take them by the scruff of their necks and propel them into one another's company and they will have to get on together as best they may. Their chances of forming a harmonious relationship will not obviously be improved by a ten-year apprenticeship of mutual avoidance; but during the years of apartheid, as long as no other factors intervene, they are free to choose the playmates with whom they have most in common.

Children are the beneficiaries of the intricate biological processes which gave them the gift of life, and for years they are biologically at liberty to exist in their own right.

Their endocrine systems are geared to serve their own interests as individual animals, to help them survive and grow. They are thus allowed—for a longer stretch of time than other primates—to relate to the world around them as if they were biological end products.

At puberty this ceases to be the case. Notice is served on them that they are not after all end products, but merely channels. Changes take place in their bodies and minds which are by no means geared to further their own survival and well-being, but which enable them to repay a debt by passing on the gift of life to a new generation. They may choose not to exercise this ability, but they are subjected (whether they like it or not) to the powerful behavioural, emotional and psychological pressures which sexually mature flesh is heir to.

Children are sometimes told about the wonderful prospects which will open up for them one day when they become 'grown-up'. They can be forgiven if, in surveying the antics of some who have already attained that goal, they occasionally have their doubts. Poets remember those misgivings. Wordsworth described how:

> Shades of the prison house begin to close
> Upon the growing boy,

and Longfellow wrote of the young maiden:

> Standing with reluctant feet
> Where the brook and river meet.

That is the point at which, for the purpose of this book, we take leave of them. Good luck to them all. They're going to need it.

23

Light on the Past

For scientists, as for children, one of the most exciting questions is 'Why?' and the central mystery in anthropology is why humans are so different from the African apes, despite the fact that we are so closely related to them. To a Darwinian, this means that they must at some time have become adapted by natural selection to life in a different kind of environment from the forest-dwelling apes.

For over fifty years students of human evolution have been following a trail which initially looked very promising, but it has led them nowhere and has finally petered out. It began in the 1920s when Raymond Dart brilliantly identified the fossil skull of a young primate as a hominid.

Since the skull had been discovered on the African savannah, Dart was led to believe that the savannah was the true cradle of humankind. Once the hominid status of the Taung skull had been authenticated, his theory was taken up with enthusiasm and rapidly became the new orthodoxy. The hypothesis suggested that the African forests shrank, and some apes were forced out onto the more challenging habitat of the grasslands. There they lost their fur to keep cool, evolved bigger brains to fashion tools and weapons, ran on two legs to chase after game, and learned to speak in order to plan their hunting strategies and pass on their tool-making skills.

The central weakness of this scenario has always been that other primates—baboons, vervet monkeys, geladas, patas monkeys, savannah chimpanzees—have also left the forest to live on the savannah. Some of them have been there for millions of years. But none of them has ever acquired—not even in incipient form—a single one of the characteristics which distinguish humans from apes. They have all remained hairy and quadrupedal and unable to speak.

In recent years it has become clear that the imagined sequence of events basic to savannah theory was incorrect. We now know from the fossil evidence that bipedalism was well established by 3.7 million years ago, and therefore must have been embarked on considerably earlier, while the savannah ecosystem did not emerge until around two-and-a-half million years ago. Careful examination has been carried out of fossilised pollen grains and the fossilised bones of grazing animals and of the smaller mammals that lived in the areas now designated as savannah. It has been shown that before two-and-a-half million years ago the flora and fauna were typical of wooded areas rather than grasslands. The great explosion in the variety of different grazing species, as Elizabeth Vrba pointed out, began at around that date. Richard Leakey has summed up the implication of these discoveries: 'In fact, the great plains and the immense herds on them are relatively recent aspects of the African environment, much more recent than the origin of the human family.'

Since the move to the savannah has so long been held to be the whole *raison d'être* of the process of humanisation, this new scenario has been difficult to assimilate. Descriptions of the environment of the early australopithecines have had to be modified. But the forests were by that time beginning to be broken up by clearings and stretches of open country, and this is felt to justify the retention of the magic word: it was 'savannah forest' or 'savannah mosaic'.

So, just as if nothing had happened, the orthodox explanations of features such as bipedalism and hairlessness continue to be described in terms of adaptations to the scorching heat of the open plains, the meagre vegetation and the scarcity of water.

This implies that the brief exposure to sunlight involved in occasionally crossing the open spaces was so traumatic that our ancestors were forced to change their life-style, shed their fur and transform their age-old modes of locomotion, thermoregulation and communication in ways no other primate has ever done. That is highly improbable. What proportion of open space to forest would be necessary to compel an ape to evolve such dras-tic adaptations? Twenty-five per cent grassland? Fifty per cent? As it happens, we have a clue to the answer. There is a well-established colony of chimpanzees in Senegal, occupying a habitat of which only five per cent is wooded. They show every sign of having adapted to that environ-ment as successfully as all the other savannah primates have done, and with just as little incentive to become bald or walk on their hind legs.

The only serious alternative to the moribund savannah theory is the Aquatic Ape Theory (AAT). A detailed account of the evidence in its favour is given in *The Scars of Evolution*. A brief outline is necessary here before con-sidering what bearing it might have on the evolution of the child.

At around the time of the split from the apes, and before the African forests gave way to savannah, there was one major and dramatic environmental event at the northern end of the Rift Valley. A large area of what is now conti-nental Africa—corresponding to the low-lying land known as the Afar Triangle—was flooded by the sea, in a geological upheaval caused by the jostling of three conti-nental plates which converge in that area. It remained flooded for hundreds of thousands of years, until it became land-locked at the eastern side and began to evap-orate, as the Dead Sea is doing now, leaving a vast salt plain.

That area of Africa was part of a wide belt of tropical

forest crossing North Africa and Asia. The AAT proposes that some of the indigenous apes living in that region could have been cut off from the rest of the ape population and forced to adapt to a semi-aquatic life in flood plains or coastal marshlands or off-shore islands for up to a million years. Finally the drying up of the sea of Afar caused them to follow the waterways of the Rift Valley upstream and inland to the riverside and lakeside sites where virtually all of the African hominid fossils have been discovered.

The strongest evidence in support of AAT is anatomical. A list can be drawn up of all the physical features distinguishing humans from apes—such features as the loss of body hair, subcutaneous fat, face-to-face copulation, the shedding of tears, the hymen, volitional breath control, the diminution of apocrine glands, the migration of the vagina to a sheltered site within the body wall, and the descended larynx. None of these features is found in savannah mammals. But examples of all of them can be found among those species of mammals which have adapted to aquatic or semi-aquatic life, such as whales and dolphins, seals and sealions, manatees, hippopotamuses, otters and beavers.

In the context of this book the question is whether a semi-aquatic stage in the evolution of humans would offer a possible explanation for some of the anomalous features of our offspring, before and after birth—the vernix caseosa, the shedding of the lanugo, the fat layer, bipedalism, speech and brain growth.

The one thing that is clear about the vernix is that it is composed of sebum secreted by the sebaceous glands. The only known function of sebum is waterproofing. It is not needed to protect the skin of the fetus against the amniotic fluid—otherwise it would be essential to the fetuses of all mammals, and there are many species of mammals including, for example, most of the rodents, which have no sebaceous glands on their bodies.

If an ancestral hominid had had to adapt to more aquatic

surroundings as suggested, it would in the first instance have ventured into water while still covered with fur. As V. E. Sokolov points out in his account of skin adaptations in aquatic mammals, one of the characteristics of furred aquatic mammals such as otters and beavers and water voles is that 'the sebaceous and sweat glands are commonly large. Their secretion lubricates the pelage and is largely responsible for keeping it dry and water-repellent.' In the same way, aquatic birds like petrels and pelicans secrete far more oil for preening than land birds do. It would appear to be one of the earliest ways of adapting to a semi-aquatic environment.

In the human fetus the sebaceous glands become active when the coat of silky prenatal hair (the lanugo) first appears—conceivably a recapitulation of the first ancestral adaptation to the water. As the lanugo becomes sparser, the vernix that remains is thickest in those areas where there is still hair—on the scalp and the eyebrows and the eyelashes. When all the lanugo has gone, the vernix too begins to disappear, though it is usually still in evidence at birth.

In the large aquatic mammals stage two of the adaptation to the water is dispensing with body hair altogether, as in dolphins and seacows and hippopotamuses; this stage also is recapitulated in the unborn human when it sheds the lanugo.

The suggested savannah explanations for hairlessness are that it was a device for cooling the ancestral hominid when it became overheated. As Professor J.Z. Young remarked, 'This explanation is not very convincing for such a striking condition.' His comment on the aquatic theory as early as the 1970s was, 'Many human features are compatible with this possibility, but it is difficult to find direct evidence for it (or against it either!).'

One reason why the cooling-down hypothesis is unconvincing is that shaving any of the fur or hair from an animal in the tropics results in its body temperature going up, not down. The other savannah explanation is the assertion that when the hominid adopted sweat-cooling it was necessary to become naked to allow the sweat to evaporate. However, the patas monkey, the fastest running primate in the savannah, uses sweat-cooling very efficiently without requiring hairlessness to make it effective.

Apart from fossorial (that is, underground) mammals, the only naked mammals are those that are aquatic or semi-aquatic, or have been so in the past. The naked animals found today on the savannah are humans and pachyderms—the thick-skinned wallowing species like the hippopotamus and the rhino and the elephant. The elephant comes from a very ancient line; it has several features which it shares with aquatic mammals, including a kind of long-distance sonar communication, which it shares with the whales, originating from the region of its forehead. The most detailed and up-to-date evolutionary study of the elephant and its ancestors is by M.S. Fisher and P. Tass, and it concludes: 'We assume a semi-aquatic ancestry for the Tethytheria' (the group which includes the elephant and the seacow). In other words, the reason why the elephants, like humans, have so many unique and puzzling features is because they are palinosts—animals which, after adapting for a long period to a new and strange environment, ultimately return to a previous one. This course of events is not as rare as is sometimes assumed. All snakes, for example, are palinosts— descended from four-legged creatures that adapted to a burrowing life and became totally streamlined before later returning to live above ground.

The next anomalous event in human prenatal development is the heavy investment during the last weeks of pregnancy in a thick layer of subcutaneous fat. Like the naked skin, this is very common among aquatic mammals, but very rare in terrestrial ones. Land animals which do store fat are hibernators, like the hedgehog: they store it up in autumn in order to live off it while they sleep away the winter. In humans, however, the layer is not seasonal. Some primates become obese in old age in captivity, but none of them gives birth to fat babies. That would be dangerously maladaptive, constituting an extra hazard for mothers whether swinging through the trees or escaping predators on the savannah.

Only in an aquatic environment would a fat baby be less burdensome than a thin one, because one of the functions of fat in aquatic mammals is to give buoyancy. A young baby which has been accustomed to the water from an early age will float happily and unsupported in a pool, whereas an ape or monkey of the same age—with its large proportion of lean tissue—would drown. In some lakeside tribes mothers are well aware of this: when they are busy fishing or washing clothes, a fretful infant may be put down into the water as casually and safely as a Western mother would put it down into a cot.

Terrestrial mammals occasionally put on weight in a good season, but any fat laid down for storage is usually deposited in internal sites: most of a human baby's fat— like that of all aquatic mammals, is immediately under the skin. In addition to its amount and its location, there is a third feature which is very rare in land mammals. Non-human species sometimes acquire deposits of fat in a few sites under the skin and, as previously observed, the fat is attached to the underlying tissue so that the skin slides easily over it; in humans, and in all aquatic mammals, the subcutaneous fat is bonded to the skin: when the skin moves, the fat moves with it.

In attempting to reconstruct the course of events, scientists are handicapped by the fact that the only changes that can be dated—even approximately—are changes affecting the skeleton. Soft tissues do not fossilise, so we cannot know whether the hominids became naked at the same time as they became bipedal.

However, since in the course of our evolution extraordinary things happened to the pelvis and the skin and the hair and the respiratory canal, it would be more parsimonious to assume that they happened at the same time. Otherwise, we have to postulate one set of unusual environmental events causing skeletal changes, and a series of other quite separate environmental events accounting for nakedness, subcutaneous fat, the descent of the larynx, and so on.

It has already been pointed out that a semi-aquatic phase in human evolution may have been conducive to nakedness and subcutaneous fat. It remains to be considered whether the same thing might be true of bipedalism, bigger babies, and brain growth, and speech.

With regard to bipedalism, all scientists now agree that purely as a means of getting from A to B, incipient bipedalism would have been so inefficient that it must have bestowed some non-locomotive advantage or it would never have evolved. As long ago as 1960 Alister Hardy argued that bipedalism could well have evolved in response to the necessity of wading through water. Proboscis monkeys in the swamps of Borneo regularly wade bipedally through the streams and backwaters carrying their babies. Constant practice has so accustomed them to it that deeper in the forest bands of them can be seen walking bipedally on land. The only extant ape living in a somewhat similar environment is the pygmy chimpanzee (the bonobo), whose core habitat consists of swamps and seasonally flooded forests. It stands up straighter than other chimpanzees; its limb proportions strikingly resemble those of Lucy. Bonobos in zoos certainly walk bipedally more frequently than other African apes, and they frequently copulate face-to-face.

There are three possible links between the Aquatic Ape Theory and brain growth. They concern the adequacy of the diet, the nutritional balance of the diet, and the means of locomotion.

Some versions of the savannah theory have centred

around the question of diet, arguing that with a change of habitat the protohominids would have had to seek new means of subsistence: they may have become scavengers, or seed eaters or hunters. The hunting hypothesis, long the most popular, has lost support since the discovery of bipedal hominids dating long before there is any evidence of tools or weapons. And the other options refer to food resources that are either chancy, or seasonal, or arduous to collect in large enough quantities. In all cases this would afford a more meagre and less reliable food supply than the forest apes can depend on.

In reality, as stressed by R.D. Martin, the change must have been to a more nourishing and reliable food source. That alone would enable the females to produce heavier babies with bigger brains, and to feed them for the next few years with milk rich and plentiful enough to fuel the continued rapid brain growth and the fat layer.

If the protohominids at the time of the split turned to the sea instead of the savannah for sustenance, the increased supply of nourishment would be freely available. Coastal waters in tropical latitudes sustain the highest biomass of any environment on the planet.

Michael Crawford has made the further point that building brain tissue imposes special requirements that do not apply to other body tissues—it demands a one-to-one balance between Omega-6 and Omega-3 fatty acids. Omega-3 fatty acids are relatively scarce in the land food chain, but predominate in the marine food chain.

While the connection between brain growth and nutrition is by now well understood in scientific circles, the connection between brain growth and locomotion is less familiar.

In 1981 John. E. Eisenberg published a book called *The Mammalian Radiations*, reviewing the history of mammals and analysing trends in their evolution, adaptation and behaviour. In a chapter on encephalisation (increase in relative brain size) he constructed a table correlating brain size and mode of locomotion in mammals and commented:

> One will note that complex locomotor patterns involving movement in three different directions, such as arboreality or aquatic adaptations, are strongly associated with high encephalisation quotients, whereas movements in essentially two dimensions generally is associated with a lower encephalisation quotient.

This would explain why all primates, being originally arboreal, have slightly bigger brains than most non-primate species. This correlation would lead us to expect that an arboreal primate descending to the two-dimensional world of the savannah would have lesser needs in respect of brain size. But locomotion in water—swimming and diving—is three-dimensional and, other things being equal, it would tend to lead to higher encephalisation.

Learning to speak needed more than increased cranial capacity. There were two other prerequisites, not obviously connected with one another but both connected with aquatic environments.

The first was voluntary breath control. Young children acquire this early in life; they delight in practising the new skill, and sometimes frighten their parents by deliberately holding their breath for long periods. They are also practising it when they begin to babble. Voluntary breath control is found in all diving birds and diving mammals, but in no terrestrial ones.

The second was the descended larynx which enables a human child to produce a greater variety of sounds than a young chimpanzee is capable of. The descended larynx is found in a few aquatic mammals—the sirenians (sea-cows) and the sealion—but in no terrestrial ones.

A baby acquires this double increase over the command of his utterances at a time when his mind is still unstructured. He is registering incoming stimuli—sights and smells and sounds and faces—discovering that some are related to one another and to his own bodily sensations. He is laying down connections between these things which partly dictate the way his mind will work for the rest of his life. His own voice, and his ability to control it before he can properly control his limbs, is one item in the newly dealt pack of data with which he has to deal.

At some time, in somebody's brain, somewhere in the world, an unprecedented connection was laid down—a connection between a vocal syllable and an object. A common hypothesis is that it was probably an alpha male who sat down and pondered, reflecting that there must be a more efficient method of interpersonal communication than body language, and if only he could devise one it would fulfil a long felt want. That is unlikely. He would have had more forceful, tried and tested ways of fulfilling his wants, and he would have been set in his ways.

It could have been an infant, shuffling the newly dealt pack of internal sensations and incoming data in a brain still unstructured, coming up with a new combination, with no way of knowing it was newer than any of the others, making a connection between a lusted-after object in his line of vision and a sound coming out of his babbling mouth. It could have been his mother watching him who perceived the way his mind was working and understood the syllable and fed it back to him. That would have made it into a word. There has to be some reason why the girls, throughout evolution the baby-rearers, are quicker at picking up the trick of language than the boys.

As for the slowing down of the rate at which we live our lives, it is difficult to find any evidence of where or why it might have happened. There is one indication that it did not happen on the savannah. If our ancestors had moved from trees to savannah, their life clocks would have speeded up rather than slowing down. A paper by C.R. Ross in 1988 compared the life histories of tropical rain forest primates with those of savannah primates, and discovered that relative to body size the forest primates without exception lived at a slower rate.

It appears to be true that aquatic mammals tend to lead slower lives than terrestrial ones, but that is largely because they are bigger. They can afford to grow bigger because, in the low-gravity medium of water, added weight is cost-free in energy terms. The great whales are bigger than the largest dinosaurs. But their metabolic rate—unlike ours—is no slower than would be expected in view of their size.

There is just one unexpected possible connection between slowing down and water which is independent of body size. Unfortunately there is a snag in it.

In 1966 C.F. Kelly and A.H. Smith reported to NASA their findings that when they subjected growing chicks to an experimental increase in the accelerative field by the use of centrifuge—in effect, subjecting them to increased gravitational pull—two consequences were observed: retarded growth and increased metabolic rate. In purely theoretical terms it should follow that *decreasing* the pull of gravity should have the opposite effect—speeding up the rate of growth and slowing down the rate of development.

That is exactly what has happened to the human fetus. And on our planet, the only environment where the pull of gravity is drastically reduced is in water. That is an intriguing thought—undermined, alas, by the consideration that all mammalian fetuses develop in a gravity-free aquatic medium, whatever kind of environment their mothers inhabit.

'Changes in the child,' according to the *Encyclopaedia Britannica* 'are so striking that it is almost as if the child were a series of distinct yet related individuals as he passes through infancy, childhood and adolescence'. Through all the vicissitudes of the last five million years those other smaller phenotypes of our species have accompanied us every step of the way. Each one of us, like every one of our ancestors, has passed through, and been moulded by, those vital stages of the human life cycle.

For some of the costlier features which we have come to regard as triumphs, such as the combination of the erect stance and the big brain, the price has disproportionately been paid by the mother/infant dyad. When problems arose, the incompatibility between the best solution for the adult female and the best solution for the child resulted in a kind of makeshift physical compromise, the key to which was the immature delivery of the fetus. Neither side could win at too great a cost to the other if the species was to survive. The story of evolution is not about how a species finds a perfect solution to its problems. A species can be modified by natural selection, but the modification can never involve going back to scratch and starting again. What any species ends up with is the best solution available, considering all the irrelevant obsolescent physical and mental baggage it has to drag around from the distant past.

It now looks as if we are approaching another of the critical turning points in our evolutionary and social history. The underlying tensions between the individual interests of mother and child have been partly obscured and partly held in equilibrium by the emergence over the millennia of an institution known as the nuclear family. Until well into the present century there was a widespread assumption that this was an immutable part of our genetic inheritance.

In the light of recent developments it appears far from immutable. The consequences are all around us, and people are asking one another: 'Where will it all end? What about the children? What are we going to do?'

24

The Family

For most of the five million years of separate existence, the evolution of the line leading to *Homo sapiens* has been governed by precisely the same rules as that of all other mammals. The rules are that any inadequacy or any behaviour pattern which militates against the production and successful rearing of a new generation is weeded out by natural selection. Males that fail to copulate, females that fail to take adequate care of their offspring leave no copies of themselves behind them. The system works well, but is predicated on two assumptions—that copulation is followed by reproduction and that only the fittest will survive.

In our own species in more recent times these assumptions have been undermined. We have learned how to manipulate our environment so that the unfit also survive; and we indulge in dysgenic behaviour like making war, in which the young and healthy are preferentially sacrificed and no amount of physical or mental fitness lessens their chance of being killed by machines. We have also found ways to ensure that copulation is not followed by reproduction, and even to arrange that reproduction is not preceded by copulation. In these and other ways we have thrown a spanner into the works of natural selection and are into an entirely new ball game.

Much of the unease about current social changes is centred around the institution of the nuclear family which is perceived to be under threat. There are some who would welcome its demise and others who regard that outcome as disastrous, especially for the children. There is a general impression on both sides that the weakening of the family was instigated by propaganda from liberals and feminists, and that it might be combated by exhortations to return to older values.

But such opinions, and the readiness to listen to them, are the symptoms rather than the causes of deeper underlying changes. Some of the questions that need to be considered are why the institution of the nuclear family arose, what were the strengths that kept it in being so long, and what is undermining it now.

There were two reasons why people believed that the nuclear family as the basic unit of human society had existed for millions of years. It was partly because people found it hard to envisage a society of bipeds organised in any other way, and partly because in the heyday of the savannah theory it seemed to offer an explanation of bipedalism. The theory was that the male ranged at large over the savannah and returned on two legs to free his hands for carrying food back to base, to his mate and their children. There is no evidence that four million years ago there ever was such a base, or that it would have been wise to leave females and young unprotected there, or that for a quadruped it would be more efficient to carry things back to them on two legs, or that the first hominids had any more reason than any other African primates to become monogamous.

In mammals, the oldest of all the social bonds is that between mother and offspring. Compared with that, any lasting bond between a male and a female is recent and rare. In most species mating is a brief encounter, often confined to a special time of the year, and after consummation the sexes instantly lose interest in one another and go their separate ways.

The nuclear family arrangement—that is, monogamy

coupled with some paternal input into rearing the young—is unknown in any other members of the primate order to which we belong. Marmosets were at one time credited with being good fathers because females had been seen handing over their twins to be looked after while they went off to feed. But closer studies by David Abbott and Leslie Digby indicate that the mother's helpers are not the fathers, but subordinate females who are, as in the case of hyenas, discouraged from breeding themselves. The only monogamous ape is the gibbon, and he takes no interest in his offspring except to chase his sons out of his territory when they approach puberty. Among the African apes, the gorilla has a harem-type social organisation and the chimpanzees are promiscuous.

When a 'nuclear family' does arise in a mammalian species, it is driven by the needs of the offspring and the female's inability to cope on her own. Among wolves, for instance, a female normally joins in the chase after big game. It would not be practicable for her to do this when she was the mother of new-born cubs. Such chases are not only exhausting but unpredictable in distance and duration. So until the litter is older, the male brings food back to the lair.

If we assume that there was in our species a drift in the direction of pair-bonding and paternal involvement, it is unlikely to have begun earlier than two-and-a-half million years ago. That seems to have been the point at which the babies began to be slower growing; the task of caring for them would become more exacting. It was also the point at which we first find evidence of tools and weapons. At least part of the diet may have been derived from hunting, and the pattern of a gender-based division of labour as between hunting and gathering may have had its first beginnings then.

However, compared with genuinely pair-bonded species like geese and wolves, the human instinct for life-long monogamy has not been very securely established.

Some anthropologists would argue that it has not become established at all. In surveying the social mores of all the different cultures of the world they find many different kinds of social arrangement—polygamy (more than one wife), polyandry (more than one husband) and a wide variety of kinship structures. By counting cultures rather than counting heads, the nuclear family option is the exception among humans rather than the rule. And the existing state of affairs in many Western countries where around half the marriages end in divorce (and possible remarriage) has been given a label of its own: serial monogamy. It would seem that an institution so labile must be purely a matter of tradition and convention rather than any kind of genetic predisposition.

The only evidence that there has been at some point at least an incipient trend towards pair-bonding lies in the fact that people fall in love. This phenomenon, which looms so large on the literature shelves of the public library, rates scarcely a mention in the science section because it is so unquantifiable that it is hard for a scientist to get a handle on it, let alone write a thesis on it.

However, it is an observable phenomenon. Among chimpanzees it is on record than an alpha male may, over a period of days, cease to be promiscuous and spend a disproportionate amount of time in the company of a particular female while she is in oestrus. That is a well-known behaviour pattern known as 'consortship'. It is also a well-known behaviour pattern that many—perhaps most—humans at some time or other, either once or repeatedly, are subject to the hallucinatory impression that there is one human being in the world on whom all their happiness depends, and that the emotion they are experiencing will last for the rest of their lives. This is known in the vernacular as 'falling in love'.

The experience is not universal, and there is undoubtedly a strong cultural component involved in the way it is manifested in different societies, encouraged or discouraged, suppressed or faked. But it is common enough to suggest that if this behaviour was observed in any other animal it would be assumed to be part of the genetically inherited repertoire of the species.

However, this amounts to no more than a tentative development in the direction of monogamy. Humans are not in the same league as geese or timber wolves, who never experience the slightest stirring of interest in any partner other than the one they are bonded to. The strength of the institution of the nuclear family did not depend on that rather rickety biological basis. It was strong because it was buttressed by economic considerations and underwritten by the sanctions of tradition and religion.

It was not a plot for the enslavement of women. The division of labour was a thoroughly sound idea. It made perfect economic sense for women, the child bearers, to do the gathering while men did the hunting. The introduction of agriculture gave a further boost to a durable one-male/one-female relationship. A man needed extra hands to help him work his land: who more biddable than his sons? so he needed a wife.

In the era of the Industrial Revolution its rationale was stronger than ever. The men went into the factories and mines and foundries; the women had to be at home to look after the babies. The question of who would do the washing and cooking and cleaning was not worth asking. There was only one possible answer. The main beneficiaries of the permanence of this arrangement were the women and children, and women were far more anxious than men to enter into the bonds of marriage. They were infinitely worse off outside it.

The first women to question their position in society came from the more prosperous levels of society. A few of them—a scattered few—began to ask why their sex was treated as inferior. Why were they not allowed to vote? Why were women undereducated, underprivileged, legally disadvantaged, underpaid? The first answers they received were simply expressions of bigotry and prejudice: 'Because women are weak, because they are hysterical, because they are stupid'. But there was also the one answer which could not be so easily laughed off: 'Because of the children.'

All the great revolutions in history have taken place, not when the conditions of an underprivileged sector of society are at their worst, but at a time when a slight improvement in their situation leaves them a space for hope and an access of energy.

At the turn of the century two things were happening that affected women in countries like Britain and America. One was an expansion in the service industries, creating a new grade of white collar jobs which young ladies could perform as well as young gentlemen, and were willing to do more cheaply. The other was birth control. Among the better informed women, knowledge of this was spreading decades before the advent of Marie Stopes (though nobody told Queen Victoria), and families near the top of the social scale were getting smaller.

The first wave of the women's movement campaigned for things like the right to vote, the right to university education, the right of married women to own their own property instead of it all passing into their husband's possession on their wedding day, the right to become doctors. They had no intention of attacking the institution of marriage as such. Only a few wild theorists like Bernard Shaw were iconoclastic about it, claiming that the Home was 'the girl's prison and the woman's workhouse'.

All that most women wanted was more equal status within marriage, the right to divorce if the marriage became intolerable, and a chance to earn their own living with dignity if they chose to remain single.

The second wave of the women's movement, in the 1970s, was a different matter altogether. Some were campaigning over issues like equal pay and parity of esteem, and entry into the remaining bastions of male privilege, such as government and science and the priesthood. But some were issuing wholesale denunciation of institutions such as marriage and the nuclear family, and of males as a sex. A woman, they said, needs a man like a fish needs a bicycle. Women can go it alone. Many of them were already doing so, because after the Second World War, by which time the right to divorce was well established, the proportion of marriages deemed to be intolerable, either by the husband or the wife, was inexorably rising. Monogamy was on the way to becoming 'serial monogamy', one step back towards the chimpanzee's brief 'consortship'.

In those heady days the New Woman—liberated woman—was not envisaged as a person with a child in a pushchair and another clinging to her skirts. She was standing alone and elated on her own two feet with the wind in her hair, and the children had somehow been air-brushed out of the picture.

But in the real world they have never gone away, and they are not about to. They will always be there, with their big reproachful eyes, expecting to be brought up. Our future depends very largely upon how well that job is going to be done, and by whom, because in a decade or two they will be running the world we are living in.

25

The New Child

In an era of rapid social change two phrases have come into common use. There has been much talk of the New Woman, and only slightly less about the New Man. No one has yet begun speaking of the progeny of this couple as the New Child.

It has been forecast that in Britain at some time in 1994 a watershed will be passed. By the end of the year there will be more women in work than there are men in work. At the same time the predicted failure rate of marriages is around 50 per cent, and rising. Any social planning for the future must depend on whether these trends are regarded as irreversible, or whether they can and/or should be erased by moral exhortations to the people to return to their old ways.

It is very unlikely that these changes are going to be reversed. In the first place, the technical and economic changes which brought women into the work force are still in operation. Fewer and fewer jobs in the labour market now depend on muscular strength, and in the jobs that do not, women tend to be equally capable, more docile, manually more dexterous and cheaper. The extent of women's contribution to the economy has always been dictated far more by supply and demand than by their own aspirations. In wartime Britain they were advised, urged and finally conscripted to perform the jobs vacated by servicemen. Earlier in Lancashire, before feminism was heard of, the demand for cotton weavers was insatiable and for several generations working women were the social norm there. They were seldom condemned for neglecting their homes and families, but praised for their contribution to the prosperity of the nation.

Besides, many women had wanted to get into the labour market, and most of them still want to stay there. Running a house in the era of central heating, washing machines and fast food is hardly a full-time job for an able bodied adult. It is true that things have not worked out quite as they once hoped. The idea was that men would agree to perform half of the housework, and that employers would compete with one another to introduce flexitime and install crêches, but changes in these directions have been painfully slow—in fact, up to the present, barely perceptible.

Nevertheless, women have found that earning a wage or a salary gives them a degree of confidence and independence that they would be reluctant to lose. And they do not always have a choice. As soon as two-income families became the norm, prices and expectations rose to adjust to the situation. A woman in a family with a two-income mortgage, or with a husband who is unemployed or has decamped, finds that her route into the labour market has turned out to be a one-way street.

As for the divorce rate, the point has been passed when social or religious pressures were sufficient to induce couples to stay together through the bad patches in their relationship. The fear of hell fire has been removed, and when a couple splits up it is no longer a sensation or a scandal, merely a matter of 'Join the Club'. Increasingly, live-in partners avoid the complications attendant on divorce by not getting married in the first place.

This situation could be regarded as the latest example of parent/infant conflict. The breakup of the nuclear family is contrary to the wishes of the infant in whose interest it had originally come into being.

Some people try to convince themselves that there is no conflict. They say they are acting in the best interests of their youngsters—that children are better off with a single parent than with two parents who are unhappy together or constantly bickering. They say it will be better for the children as they grow up to have a fulfilled and interesting mother they can be proud of, rather than a boring one with fewer things to talk about.

The uncomfortable truth is that these claims cannot be sustained. When children are old enough to be consulted and are asked for their opinion, they make it clear that they would prefer their parents to stay together whether they are happy together or not. And a young child does not want a mother with a well stocked mind and a wide range of interests. He wants one who sticks around and is interested, as exclusively as possible, in *him*—and in him as he is now, not as he might be in fifteen years' time.

There is, of course, nothing the children can do about this: children have lost their evolutionary clout. Before *Homo* became *sapiens*, the maternal instinct was strongly selected for. The genes of females averse to baby care would have been weeded out by natural selection because their babies would have died. But that has ceased to be true. At the top end of the social scale this work has traditionally been delegated, so that a female member of a wealthy dynasty may be descended from generation after generation of women in whom any maternal instinct was as dead as a dodo. A poor mother, who is equally lacking in the wish or the ability to care for her children, may be charged with neglect and her children taken into care. They, too, will survive. She may not found a dynasty; but she could initiate a cycle of deprivation that will spin on down the generations.

The conclusion seems to be that the majority of the New Children will not be reared in the theoretical standard-model nuclear family of father, mother and 2.4 children. This thought is very alarming to people who have experienced or read about psychoanalysis and have absorbed the idea that if anyone is neurotic, aggressive, anxious or depressed, their state of mind can be traced back to something that went wrong in their infancy. They feel that any departure from the standard model may represent 'something wrong'.

One thing about psychiatrists is that in dealing with their patients they perforce begin at the end and work backwards. And the end point they start from is usually that of adults who have come to them because they are mentally disturbed. In other branches of medicine good diagnosticians normally use control groups to test their hypotheses. But it is rare to hear of a psychiatrist enrolling panels of volunteers who feel perfectly sane and well balanced, and delving back into their memories of infancy to find out whether any of *them*—and, if so, what percentage—ever felt jealous, rebuffed, or unappreciated, or saw something nasty in the woodshed at the age of six.

The point was lucidly made by N. Blurton Jones in 1993 when he compared the different approaches of psychologists and anthropologists respectively.

'Psychologists,' he wrote, 'emphasise the importance to the child's development of contingent responsiveness, sensitivity to the child's moods and signals, face-to-face interaction, a stable caretaker, conversation with adults, a stimulating environment, and firm but kindly discipline. Anthropologists point out how often children are cared for by children, how little they receive direct instruction by adults, and how scarce is face-to-face interaction between mother and infant in many cultures. Yet the children nevertheless grow up healthy, sane, and successful.'

His paper contrasted the parental behaviour of the !Kung tribe of Botswana and Namibia with that of the Hadza in north Tanzania. !Kung children have idyllic childhoods. They are not weaned until the age of four, are not expected to do any work or take responsibility for younger children, are seldom given orders or asked to run errands, are kept close to the camp for their own safety, are not punished for bad behaviour. Hazda children are weaned at two-and-a-half. They are expected to contribute to the tribe's food supply—sometimes being sent into the bush in unsupervised foraging groups where even three-year-olds may try their hands at digging—and to fetch water and firewood. If they misbehave, they are slapped and shouted at. It sounds like a recipe for producing more sullen, distrustful and aggressive children, but that is not how they are described. Blurton-Jones records that 'Hadza children lack none of the charm and imagination of !Kung children. They have a robust humour and a pride in their life that we find attractive and impressive. Some show unexpected and touching hospitality in their occasional concern that the observer should not get lost or too badly stuck in the thorns.'

The Hadza must be doing something right. Perhaps it is in the first year, when Hadza babies (like !Kung ones) spend most of their time riding on the mother's side or back. From that vantage point, apart from the comfort of the physical contact, they get a constantly changing view of the world around them, and do not need a mobile to be set up between them and the ceiling. Perhaps it is in the second and third years, when the toddler is surrounded by numbers of relatives, old, adult, and young. None of these people is likely to be in a hurry to keep the next appointment, and one or other is always prepared to take a turn at playing with the child or carrying it around. With that much attention having been paid to it in the formative years, it seems well able to cope with plenty of bawling out and bossing around when it gets older.

Those first years are basic. Every study of child (or ape) psychology confirms that the more attention and security the young are given in the beginning, the less clinging and dependent they will be when they grow older, and the more successfully they will respond to later crises and challenges. If they do not hear language spoken in their first years, they will never learn to speak it properly. If they are given nothing for their minds to work on then, that deficit cannot be made up later. If they do not experience love and trust then, later in life they may have none to give. They have very little in common with computers, but the GIGO law applies to both of them: Garbage In, Garbage Out.

Nowadays it is increasingly the case that the baby, like other sectors of the economy, is being steadily moved into the orbit of the cash nexus. It used to be the star example of a job that was carried out free of charge, and for love.

At, or near, the top of the economic scale the new system works well enough. Some early feminists sincerely recommended that 'child care is better left to the best trained practitioners', and the best trained practitioners do a good job. But in the middle income sector a woman going out to work must find someone willing to care for the baby for an amount appreciably less than she herself earns. This necessity cascades down through the wage brackets, with the result that at the lowest level daytime baby care is one of the lowest paid jobs in the whole economy. You do not get faithful retainers for that kind of money.

If the mother herself is low paid, there comes a point where she cannot afford even that. It is best for the child if, at whatever cost in material living standards, she stops trying to hold a job, and lives on social security. This makes her one of the scroungers and idlers denounced from public platforms. 'Idle' is hardly the word. She is doing a hard and important job, often as well as it can be done under appalling conditions in a high-rise flat or bed and breakfast accommodation; but she is a scrounger because it is a job society has not asked her to do. The baby may not be unwanted by its mother, but it is unwanted by society.

One quarter of Britain's children are living below the

poverty line. This is sometimes perceived as an indication that the poor breed too fast. But, as Sir William Beveridge pointed out more than fifty years ago, the poverty is not the cause of children but the result of them. At every income level parents of young children are materially worse off than their childless colleagues.

The plight of the children below the poverty line gives rise to a feeling in some people's minds that it would be better if 'people like that'—that is, poor people—did not have children. We have met with this policy in other species. It is the strategy of the hyena and the marmoset and the Cape hunting-dog: let only the alpha females bear young, and the rest of them can then be usefully employed as carers.

But *Homo sapiens* is cast in a different mould. The hankering for that solution has to be carefully wrapped up before being promoted from public platforms, because short of compulsory sterilisation there is no foolproof way of applying it. It may be pointed out that many of the mothers have acted fecklessly, and sometimes immorally (though the second epithet is apt to boomerang unless the speaker is of unimpeachable probity). It can be said that they have often brought their troubles upon themselves, and that such behaviour should not be encouraged by over-generous public aid.

The snag is that whoever has brought their troubles on their own heads is not the children. And there is no way of applying economic sanctions against the parents that will not penalise the children. In a few years' time those children will be part of our social environment. The more deprived their childhood has been—physically, mentally and socially—the less we will like the look of the particular version of the New Child that we see in the streets of our cities.

A vast amount of time, effort and money—much of it public money—is spent every year in trying to reform people after they have grown up. Reformatories, social workers, prisons, probation services, encounter groups and detention centres are all devoted to the task of trying to change one kind of person into a different kind of person. It is an arduous undertaking, like trying to make a U-turn in a narrow road with an articulated lorry. Comparatively minuscule amounts are spent on trying to influence how they grow up in the first place.

The first thing to do for them is take all possible steps to ensure that they are wanted by at least one of their parents. Some progress has been made in Britain since contraception became available on the NHS in 1974. In the twenty years up to 1991, the number of girls between fifteen and nineteen years old bearing children dropped from 71 to 42 per thousand. But there is still a long way to go: Britain still has the highest percentage of teenage single mothers in Europe, and certainly not all of those births were planned or desired.

Once the babies have arrived, they must be invested in. Many of the poverty-line children are brought up in blocks of flats which were constructed specifically for the accommodation of young low-income families, yet the needs of young children were totally ignored. The flats were often miles away from the nearest park. There was nowhere warm and dry where in the winter they could safely run about and come into contact with other children and their mothers. A single floor of a high-rise block devoted to that end—or one purpose-built centre in every housing estate—would have made the world of difference to the quality of their lives and their parents' grip on their sanity. It would be a place of their own where their presence would not be frowned on, with space and toys, with seats and coffee machines for the mothers to talk together, and an occasional half-hour of taped TV that has not been tailored to the murder-a-minute adult market.

There is only enough nursery school provision in Britain for one in three of its children. As soon as the munitions factories closed down after the War, nursery schools also closed. Where cuts have to be made, this section is treated as an obvious target of 'economies'; where manifesto promises have to be broken, this is the first to go. There should be nursery places for every child over the age of three.

The slick retort to that is: 'And where is the money to come from?' If all else fails, from lowering the compulsory school-leaving age. In too many inner city schools, money is wasted on employing teachers to stand in front of teenagers who do not want to be there, telling them things they do not want to know. The truancy rate has soared, the teachers' morale is plummeting, the system is breaking down. If 'compulsory' education ended earlier, the courses could continue to be available for such as cared to attend. The pupils would be motivated; the classes would be smaller and quieter. Resources could be channelled downward to the youngest age groups where they would make most difference, where we have not yet failed them, where it is not yet too late. The objection raised to this plan is that the teenagers who do not want to learn would be at large during term time as well as in the holidays. True. But if the State wishes to pay to have young people detained, to keep them off the streets and off the unemployment register, it should not dump that job onto the teachers and call it education.

Books about babies often stress the joy they bring into our lives. That would be easy and pleasant to do, like writing stories about the perfect romance. But too many romances are not the best preparation for the nitty-gritty of any ongoing relationship, and too much rapture is not the best preparation for coping with a child.

Along with sex education in school should go warnings not only that a baby might be conceived, but some idea of the material and psychological costs of rearing it, how it turns your life upside-down, and what a long haul it is. Joy there will certainly be: let it come as a bonus. Along with the breathing exercises in the antenatal clinic should go some counselling about what to do when the kid drives you round the bend. Young people are brought up nowadays to regard their possessions as controllable. They are sometimes affronted to discover that babies are by no means user-friendly; it is not possible to switch them off or turn the volume down, or trade them in for a different model.

The neglect or ill-treatment of babies arouses such pity and anger that it is hard to think straight about it. But after a child has been removed to safety and the perpetrators punished, it is still necessary to ask the human question 'Why?' In what lost childhood did such callousness have its roots? At what point in the cycle of deprivation would it be most expedient for society to break in and concentrate more help and more resources? There is only one possible answer.

At the beginning.

References

Aiello, L. and Dean, C. (1990). *An Introduction to Human Evolutionary Anatomy*. Academic Press.

Allen, M.L. and Lemmon, W.B. (1981). Orgasm in Female Primates. *Am. J. Primatology*. 1, 15–34.

Abitbol, M.M. (1988). Effect of posture and locomotion on energy expenditure. *Am. J. Physical Anthropology*, 77.

Blurton Jones, N. (1993). The Lives of Hunter-Gatherer Children: Effects of Parental Behaviour and Parental Reproductive Strategy. In *Juvenile Primates* (eds. Pereira, M.E. and Fairbanks, L.A.), Oxford University Press.

Blurton Jones, N. and Reynolds, V. (1978). *Human Behaviour and Adaptation*. Taylor & Francis.

Boddy, K. and Dawes, G.S. (1975). Fetal Breathing. *Br. Med. Bull.*, vol. 31, No. 1.

Bowlby, John (1980). *Attachment and Loss*. Hogarth Press.

Bromage, T.G. (1987). The biological and chronological maturation of early hominids. *J. Hum. Evol.* 16, 257–272.

Cambridge Encyclopaedia of Human Evolution (1992). Eds. Steve Jones, Robert Martin and David Pilbeam. Cambridge University Press.

Candland, D.K. (1993). *Feral Children and Clever Animals*. Oxford University Press.

Chance, M.R.A. (1988). *Social Fabrics of the Mind*. Lawrence Erlbaum Associates Ltd.

Chevalier-Skolnikoff, S. and Poirier, Frank E. (1977). *Primate Social Development*. Garland Publishing Inc.

Chodorow, N. (1978). The Reproduction of Mothering. In *Psychoanalysis and the Sociology of Gender*, University of California Press.

Clutton-Brock. T.H. (1991). *The Evolution of Parental Care*. Princeton University Press.

Crelin, E. (1973). *Functional Anatomy of the Newborn*, Yale University Press.

Davidson, P.E. (1914), *The recapitulation theory and human infancy*. Columbia University Teachers' College: New York.

Dawkins, Richard. (1976). *The Selfish Gene*. Longman.

De Waal, F. (1989). *Peacemaking among Primates*. Harvard University Press.

Eisenberg, J.F. (1981). *The Mammalian Radiations*. London: Athlone Press.

Gallup, G.G. and Suarez, D. (1983). Optimal Reproductive Strategies for Bipedalism. *J. Hum. Evol.* 12, 193–196.

Garstang, Walter. (1912). The Theory of Recapitulation: a critical reassessment. *Linnean Journal Zoology*, vol. 13, 81–101.

Gould, S.J. (1977). *Ontogeny and Phylogeny*. Harvard University Press.

Haig, David. (1993). Genetic Conflicts in Human Pregnancy. *Quarterly Review of Biology*, vol. 68, no. 4.

Hallock, M.B., Worabey, J. and Self, P.A. (1989). Behavioural Development in Chimpanzee and Human Newborns across the first month of life. *International Journal of Behavioural Development*. 12 (4), 527–540.

Hayes, Catherine (1951). *The Ape in Our House*. New York: Harper & Row.

Hofman, M.A. (1993). Encephalisation and the evolution of longevity in mammals. *J. Evol. Biol.* 6, 209–227.

Irwin, Colin (1989). The sociocultural biology of Netsilingmiut female infanticides. In *The Sociobiology of Sexual and*

Reproductive Strategies (eds. Rasa, A.E. *et al.*). Chapman & Hall.

Jonas, D.F. and Jonas, A.D. (1975). Gender Differences in Mental Function: A clue to the origin of language. *Current Anthropology*, 16, 4.

Kando, S. (ed.) (1985). *Primate Morphophysiology, Locomotor Analyses and Human Bipedalism*. University of Tokyo Press.

Kellogg, W.N. and Kellogg, L.A. (1933). *The Ape and the Child*. Hafner Publishing Company.

Kelly, C.F. and Smith, A.H. (1966). Progress report to National Aeronautic and Space Administration. NASA Publication N66-35168.

Kitzinger, Sheila (1990). *The Crying Baby*. Penguin Books.

Lee, P.C. and Bateson, P. (1986). In *Primate Ontogeny: cognition and social behaviour*. Cambridge University Press.

Leutenegger, W. (1974). Functional Aspects of Pelvic Morphology in Simian Primates. *J. Hum. Evol.* 3, 207–222.

Lewis, Jane. (1984). *Women in England, 1870–1950*. Wheatsheaf Books Ltd.

Lynch, G., Hechtel, S. and Jacobs, D. (1983). Neonate size and evolution of brain size in the Anthropoid Primates. *J. Hum. Evol.* 12, 519–522.

Maccombe, E.E. and Jacklin, C.N. (1974). *The Psychology of Sex Differences*. Stanford University Press.

Margolis, L. and Sagan, D. (1986). *The Origins of Sex: 3 billion years of genetic recombination*. Yale University Press.

Martin, R.D. (1983). Human brain evolution in an ecological context. *Am. Mus. Nat. Hist.*

Montagna, William (1982). The Evolution of Human Skin. In *Advanced Views in Primate Biology*, Springer Verlag.

Montagner, H. (1978). *L'enfant et la communication*. Paris: Stock.

Morgan, Elaine (1972). *The Descent of Woman*. London: Souvenir Press.

Morgan, Elaine (1982). *The Aquatic Ape*. London: Souvenir Press.

Morgan, Elaine (1990). *The Scars of Evolution.* London: Souvenir Press.

Moore, K.L. (1977). *The Developing Human.* Philadelphia: W.B. Saunders Company.

Napier, J.R. and Napier, P.A. (1985). *The Natural History of Primates.* British Museum Press.

Northcutt, Glenn R. (1990). Ontogeny and Phylogeny: a re-evaluation of conceptual relationships. *Brain Behav. Evol.* 36, 116–146.

Palermo, D.S. (ed.) (1972). *An Ethological Study of Children's Behaviour.* Academic Press.

Reddy, J.K. and Rao, M.S. (1977). Imitation of facial and manual gestures by human neonates. *Science,* vol. 218.

Reynolds, V. (1967). *The Apes.* New York: E.P. Dutton.

Ross, C.R. The intrinsic rate of natural increase and reproductive effort in primates. *J. Zool. London,* 214, 199–219.

Rothbart, M.K. (1973). Laughter in Young Children. *Psychological Bulletin.* vol. 80, no. 3.

Savage Rumbaugh, E.S. *et al.* (1993). Language Comprehension by Ape and Child. Monograph series of the Society for Research in Child Development. 233, 58.

Schultz, A.H. (1926). Fetal growth in Man and other primates. *Quarterly Review of Biology,* vol. 1, no. 4.

Schwartz, G.C. and Rosenblum, L.A. (1983). Allometric Influences on Primate Mothers and Infants. In *Symbiosis in Parent-Offspring Interactions* (eds. Rosenblum, L.A. and Moltz, H.). Plenum Publishing Corporation.

Sokolov, V.E. (1982). *Mammal Skin.* University of California Press.

Stearns, S.C. (1976). Lifehistory Tactics: A Review of the Ideas. *The Quarterly Review of Biology,* vol. 51, no. 1.

Trivers, R.L. (1974). Parent-offspring conflict. *American Zoologist,* 14, 249–264.

Wald, G. (1958). The significance of vertebrate metamorphosis. *Science,* vol. 128, 3337.

Wallace, A.R. (1869). *The Malay Archipelago.* Reprint 1962, Dover Publications: New York.

Wallace, Marjorie (1986). *The Silent Twins*, London: Chatto & Windus.

Wood Jones, F. (1929). *Hallmarks of Mankind*. London: Edward Arnold.

Index

blastocyst 17, 29
Blurton Jones, N. 120, 179
Boddy, K. 65
body language 104, 124, 127,
128, 166
Bolk, Louis 37
bonobo (pygmy chimpanzee)
9, 45, 53, 129, 136, 163
bowel movement 91–2, 93
Bowlby, John 117, 118, 125
boys 45, 135, 153, 154
brain
areas 133
growth 48–56, 57–61, 159,
163, 164, 165
size 22, 28, 51, 53, 54, 95,
165, 168
breast feeding 13, 80, 83, 115
breasts 45–7, 94, 115
breathing 64–6, 71, 72, 89,
97–8, 131, 159, 165
Bromage, Timothy 52
Butler, Samuel vii, viii

Caesarian section 71, 72
carnivores 135
catecholamines 70, 71
celibacy 75
Chance, Michael 149
Chevalier-Skolnikoff, Suzanne
104, 123
chest 32–3
child, new 177–86
child behaviour 93–4, 179–80
childhood 178–82
chimpanzee 7, 8, 9, 22, 26, 37,
40, 43, 47, 49, 50, 51, 54,
93, 120, 121, 123, 128, 129,
131, 134, 138, 140, 145,
149, 157, 163, 165, 172, 175

Chomsky, Noam 132
clitoridectomy 9
communication 128, 133, 135,
166
see also speech, language
consortship 172, 175
contraception 80, 83, 86, 87,
88, 174, 183
copulation, face-to-face 9, 45,
159, 163
copying movements 101–2
Crawford, Michael 164
crawling 138–9
Crelin, Edmund 97
cross-mating 57
crying 96, 106, 107, 159

Dart, Raymond 53, 156
Darwin, Charles 13, 96, 97,
104, 122
Davidson, P. E. viii, 147
Dawes, G. S. 65
Dawkins, Richard 110
Deacon, T. W. 134
death, concept of 21
development of young 22–3,
25; *see also* childhood,
family
diaphragm 66
diet 164
maternal 54, 55
Digby, Leslie 171
divorce 172, 174, 175, 177
dolphins 52
duck-billed platypus 15, 45
Dyaks of Borneo 13

echidna 15
education 184
egg donation 76